PENNINE
WAY NORTH

titles so far published in this series

Cleveland Way
Offa's Dyke Path North
Offa's Dyke Path South
Pennine Way North
The Ridgeway
South West Coast Path:
Exmouth to Poole

PENNINE WAY NORTH
Bowes to Kirk Yetholm

Tony Hopkins

Photographs by Simon Warner and Tony Hopkins
General editor Michael Allaby

AURUM PRESS

COUNTRYSIDE COMMISSION · ORDNANCE SURVEY

ACKNOWLEDGEMENTS

For their advice and information, thanks to Chris Sainty of the Pennine Way Council, John Weatherall (Northumberland County Council's rights of way officer), Simon Hodgson (Durham County ranger), Brian Long of the Forestry Commission, Jim Givens (Head Warden, Northumberland National Park), Dr Geoff Singleton, and Wendy Pettigrew of the Countryside Commission. Special thanks also to Don and Sheila Stokoe for their company out on the hills.

Tony Hopkins grew up in Derby, close to the southern Pennines, and is now an official of the Northumberland National Park. He has written and illustrated several guidebooks and books of walks.

This edition first published 1989 by Aurum Press Ltd in association with the Countryside Commission and the Ordnance Survey
Text copyright © 1989 by Aurum Press Ltd, the Countryside Commission and the Ordnance Survey
Maps Crown copyright © 1989 by the Ordnance Survey
Photographs copyright © 1989 by the Countryside Commission

British Library Cataloguing in Publication Data
Hopkins, Tony
The Pennine Way North: Bowes to Kirk
Yetholm. – (National trail guides; 6)
1. England. Pennines. Long-distance
footpaths: Pennine Way. Recreations:
Walking – Visitors' guides
I. Title   II. Series
796.5'1'09428

ISBN 1 85410 018 1
OS ISBN 0 319 00174 1

Book design by Robert Updegraff
Jacket photograph: a westerly view back over Crag Lough from Hotbank Crags
Title page photograph: Shitlington Crag, south of Bellingham
Photograph of Levy Pool on page 43 (top) reproduced with the permission of Beamish North of England Open Air Museum

Typeset by Wyvern Typesetting Ltd, Bristol
Printed and bound in Italy by Printers Srl, Trento

CONTENTS

Circular walks appear on pages 36, 82, 95 and 140

How to use this guide

The 250-mile (402-kilometre) Pennine Way is covered by two national trail guides. This book features the northern section of the Way, from Bowes to Kirk Yetholm (129 miles/207 kilometres). A companion guide will feature the Way from Edale in the Peak District to Bowes.

The guide is in three parts:

1   The introduction, with an historical background to the trail and advice for walkers.

2   The Pennine Way itself, split into nine chapters, with maps opposite the description for each route section. This part of the guide also includes information on places of interest and background features as well as a number of circular walks which can be taken around each part of the Way. Key sites are numbered both in the text and on the maps to make it easier to follow the route description.

3   The last part includes useful information, such as local transport, accommodation and organisations involved with the Pennine Way.

The maps have been prepared by the Ordnance Survey for this trail guide using 1:25 000 Pathfinder or Outdoor Leisure maps as a base. The line of the Pennine Way is shown in yellow, with the status, where known, of each section of the Way – footpath, bridleway or byway, for example – shown in green underneath (see key on inside front cover). These rights of way markings also indicate the precise alignment of the Way, which walkers should follow. In some cases, the yellow line on these maps may show a route which is different from that shown on older maps; walkers are recommended to follow the yellow route in this guide, which in most cases will be the route that is waymarked with the distinctive acorn symbol ♀ used for all national trails. In a few places the author has given alternative routes to follow; full details are in the text. Any parts of the Way that may be difficult to follow on the ground are clearly highlighted in the route description, and important points to watch for are marked with letters in each chapter, both in the text and on the maps. *Some maps start on a right-hand page and continue on the left-hand page – these are identified in the text.*

Should there be a need to divert the Pennine Way from the route shown in this guide, for maintenance work or because the route has had to be changed, walkers are advised to follow the waymarks or signs.

Linear route maps at the beginning of each chapter show the principal places on or near the trail. Circled points indicate the start of a circular walk.

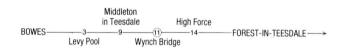

Preface

The Pennine Way is one of the national trails in England and Wales which the Countryside Commission promotes for walkers – and, in the case of some trails, for riders – to explore and enjoy the best of our countryside, far away from towns, traffic and the bustle of urban life.

The Pennine Way is special among the national trails. It was the first, remains the best-known and offers a unique experience. The original concept was a continuous walk along the high tops of the spine of England, providing a physical challenge and an experience of predominantly wild country. We intend that the Pennine Way should continue to meet that description and reward experienced walkers who are willing to endure rough going and wild moorland and who have the ability, when necessary, to steer a course by map and compass.

Over the past 25 years, however, the very popularity of this challenge has led to damage. The Pennine Way passes over some of the most fragile peat soils in England and now remedial action is necessary. Also, the original route was not ideal in places and alternatives have been promoted, unofficially as well as officially. This guide recommends the author's choice of route where there are alternatives. During the next few years we intend to work with the managers of the route (the highway authorities and national parks) to improve the Pennine Way. Future editions of this guide will show changes to the route as they are agreed, but in the meantime please help us by following any signed diversions.

We hope you will enjoy walking along the Pennine Way and that this guide will help to make your journey one to remember.

Sir Derek Barber
Chairman
Countryside Commission

PART ONE

INTRODUCTION

Life without a challenge would be a sad affair. Each day brings new opportunities and fresh experiences, and for those who enjoy weekend walking or days in the wild corners of the countryside, each step leads closer to the greatest walk of all, the Pennine Way. It is the ultimate pipe-dream, a 250-mile (400-km) path along the backbone of the land, over peaks and limitless moors, across rivers and valleys, through farms and villages.

The origins of the Pennine Way

The Pennine Way was the first national trail in Britain, officially opened on 24th April 1965, at a gathering of over 2,000 walkers at Malham Moor in the Yorkshire Dales. The project had gained Ministerial approval in 1951 but it took a further 14 years for local authorities to open up the 70 miles (113 km) of new paths necessary to complete the route.

The original idea for a continuous Pennine walk appeared in a *Daily Herald* article in 1935, written by the rambler and journalist Tom Stephenson. He had been impressed by similar trails in the United States and had the vision to apply the concept of a wilderness path to the English Pennines. The country was ready and the suggestion was carried forward on the same heady wind of change that had demanded access to the hills and the establishment of national parks. Most of the fieldwork for the Pennine Way was undertaken by the Ramblers' Association and the Youth Hostels Association in the late 1930s. The intervention of the war only sharpened the nation's appetite for peace and the appreciation of its heritage, so the 1949 Act was carried through Parliament in an atmosphere of optimism.

Forty years later millions of people walk the countryside without considering their right to be there, which is as it should be. A wind blows only when there is a vacuum to be filled. But there are still problems to be resolved. The countryside is changing fast and access is still a central issue. The Countryside Commission has announced a programme for the establishment of new national trails. The Pennine Way stands as the first and furthest of high hills walks; it is a demonstration of how people can find peace and freedom in an overcrowded age. Tom

Stephenson died in 1987, shortly after his 94th birthday. The trail-blazing has been done and the 'long green trail', sometimes blackened into a peaty groove, is there for all to follow.

How to walk the Way

Some people complete the Pennine Way in 10 days and complain afterwards that it was nothing more than an endurance test. Others take a month and return home refreshed and happy. Personal achievement is impossible to measure against time and distance. This book sets out to guide walkers along the northern half of the Way, from Bowes in County Durham to Kirk Yetholm in the Borders. It does this in nine sections; a companion volume deals with the southern half of the Way in ten sections, thus implying that the whole trail should last 19 days. This is a reasonable estimate based on a sensible itinerary, but there are many alternatives. One of the pleasures of a long walk is planning it to suit yourself. There is no obligation to start from Edale, or to do the entire distance in one go. Some natural units, such as the crossing of the Cheviots, make ideal weekend projects, and many day-length walks offer unrivalled opportunities to see high country. It is possible to build the whole trail slowly by taking it in sections separated by weeks, months or even years, or to select the most dramatic stretches and pack them into a few unforgettable days. The

The most popular breed of sheep along the Pennines is the Swaledale.

nature of the Pennines makes it difficult to find circular routes which give a true impression of the landscape, but a few are included in this book. They incorporate parts of the Way and stand on their own as good walks. Of course, nothing will quite compare with the sense of achievement, of weary exhilaration, that will come from completing the whole route as it was intended.

Landscape along the Way

Kinder and Bleaklow apart, the landscape of the northern half of the Way from Bowes to Kirk Yetholm, as described in this book, is more rugged and remote than that of the southern half from Edale to Bowes. The grey Durham moors of Bowes and Cotherstone fall away into a series of green valleys through which flow the Balder, the Lune and the Tees Rivers. After the meadows and pastures of Upper Teesdale the Way gains height until the broad cleft of High Cup, the most impressive landscape feature on the entire route, leads west into the Eden Valley. From the village of Dufton the Way begins to climb again, higher and higher until it is following the East Pennine ridge culminating in Cross Fell. A 'corpse road' then descends into the South Tyne Valley and the little town of Alston, which reflects the ebb and flow of North Pennine industries and now lies at the heart of the most extensive area of outstanding natural beauty in Britain.

North of Alston the Way flanks the South Tyne again before crossing desolate Blenkinsopp Common and arriving at Greenhead on the Tyne-Solway Gap. Here the Way enters Northumberland National Park, heading east along the Whin Sill and beside Hadrian's Wall for several miles before turning north again to cross the forests and fields of Wark and so arrive at the market town of Bellingham. The open moors and wastes of Redesdale, a wilderness created out of centuries of Border conflict, carry the Way north again only to plunge into the dark forest of Kielder. Near the head of Redesdale, Byrness marks the last settlement on the route before the curtain of forest is drawn back to reveal the Cheviot massif and the dramatic Border Ridge. Kirk Yetholm, on the banks of Bowmont Water and a few miles south-east of Kelso and the River Tweed, lies at the end of the journey.

It took millions of years to create the bedrock of the British landscape, but the effects of climate and the introduction of farming have changed the complexion of even the remotest hills

High Force in Teesdale, one of the most impressive waterfalls to be found in Britain.

High Cup, a cleft in the Pennine ridge west of the Cumbrian/Durham border.

in a fraction of that time. Seven thousand years ago most of the Pennines would have been covered in trees or scrub, but an increase in rainfall and the clearance of the primary woodland caused a build-up of peat and the beginning of mires and bogs.

The British climate has changed several times since then, but it is now in a cool and wet phase – especially in the uplands – and blanket bog pervades the Pennines as it has for centuries. The terrain of the route is variable. There are paths along river gravels and through meadows, and along dry grassy ridges with scree and rocky scrambles, but there are also long and dreary stretches of black, waterlogged peat.

Planning your walk

The Pennine Way can be a dangerous place, so preparation is important. Anyone who has never tried hill walking should test themselves over a few days or weekends in the Lake District or the Brecon Beacons before deciding to take on the Pennine Way. Many young people find they are naturally fit but lack stamina. People over 40 still have the potential for excellent stamina but lack fitness. It is never too late to get fit, but the older you are the more gentle should be the programme. Some kind of aerobic or heart and lung exercise (which gets you sweaty and breathless) for 20 minutes every two or three days is an ideal level of preparation, and can be built up gradually. If you can cope with this sort of routine, through such activities as swimming or jogging, then a day or two on the Pennine Way should hold no fears at all. However, to cope with the whole walk, day after day, requires extra stamina which can only be earned the hard way, on the hills.

The likeliest reasons for having to drop out of a long walk are blisters or sore feet. Boots should be thoroughly worn in and socks should be absorbent and without lumpy seams. Hardening the skin on the soles and heels, by applying alcohol (surgical spirit) for a few weeks before a big walk, helps to prevent blisters from forming. If they do form, prick them and apply a porous plaster which will keep the dead skin in place over the tender new layer underneath. Bruised toenails can be avoided by keeping them clipped and making sure boots fit properly in the first place.

A walker's first-aid kit should contain a few plasters, paracetamol and codeine tablets, something to treat diarrhoea, something to treat midge bites (hydrocortisone cream rather than antihistamine, which can cause a reaction) and insect repellent (e.g. oil of citronella). Lip salve can help wind-dried lips and Vaseline can soothe sore or chapped skin in unexpected parts of the body. It is a great help to know a little about first aid, and to be aware of the treatment for gastroenteritis (drink clear fluids with glucose and a little salt), exposure (glucose, warm dry clothing and a quick walk down to shelter) and adder bites (seldom fatal but should not be ignored – immobilise the affected area and seek medical advice). Most people who get into trouble on exposed sections of the Pennine Way are ill-equipped and ill-prepared.

Essential clothing for a day on the Pennines should include a set of waterproofs (cagoule and overtrousers), a pair of warm trousers and a pullover. You may not need all of these items (shorts and T-shirt may suffice on certain memorable days) but they should be packed in the rucksack just in case. Heavyweight mountain boots can be uncomfortable and may take months or years to wear in. You may prefer modern lightweight leather walking boots, with ankle support (to reduce the risk of sprained ankles) and a degree of waterproofing. They are very much better than trainers even on dry ground. Once upon a time the Pennine bogs would have rendered any footwear waterlogged within minutes, but the latest boots and yeti-gaiters have made it possible to keep your feet dry even after crossing Kinder or The Cheviot. A good rucksack deserves as much loyalty as a comfortable pair of boots. Some are top-heavy, some have narrow or slipping straps and some absorb rainwater like a sponge. Some do all these things and still cost a lot of money. Into the rucksack should go a compass and a set of appropriate maps, so don't forget this book!

Food and an adequate supply of drink (probably more than you think) and money (ditto) complete the basic list, to which can be added camera, notebook and whatever else you feel inclined to take with you. Company, or the deliberate avoidance of it, will of course be the nub of one of the most important decisions before the start of the walk. Safety, making sure someone knows where you are, is even more important for lone walkers than it is for groups.

Anyone undertaking the whole walk will also need to think carefully about accommodation, whether they are youth hostelling, bed and breakfasting or camping, for this will affect how much they carry and where they need to pick up provisions. Useful information, including a list of addresses to write to, appears on page 162.

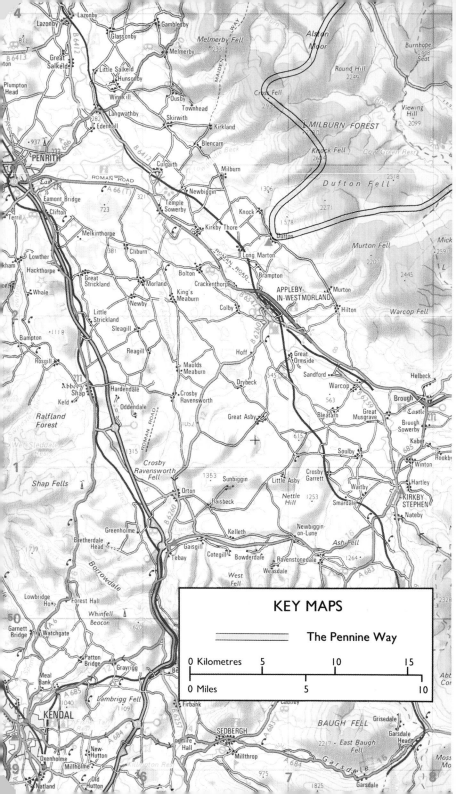

KEY MAPS

The Pennine Way

0 Kilometres 5 10 15

0 Miles 5 10

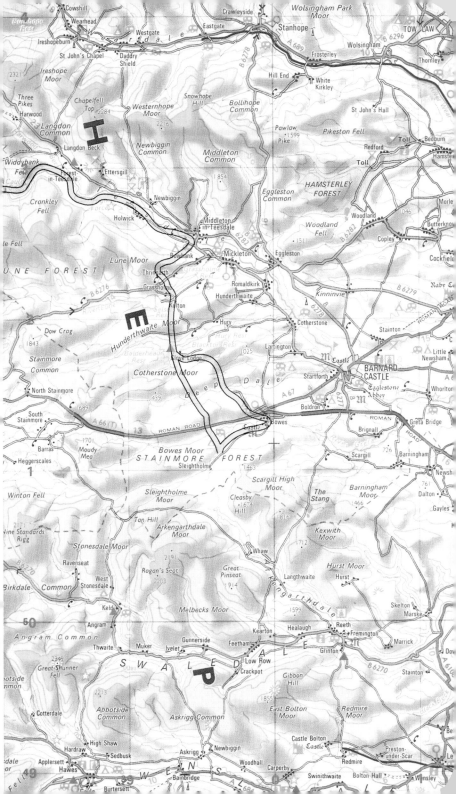

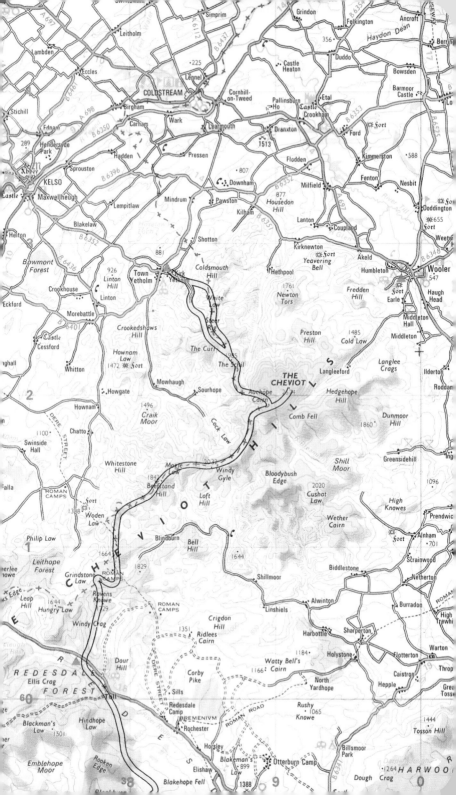

PART TWO

PENNINE WAY NORTH
Bowes to Kirk Yetholm

Bowes to Forest-in-Teesdale

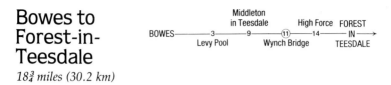

18¾ miles (30.2 km)

If you are walking direct from Keld via Tan Hill to Baldersdale, having followed the first volume of this guide, by now you will be at the A66 above God's Bridge and should continue northward following the route described below. If you are starting from Bowes or have followed the 'Bowes loop' and are continuing on to Forest-in-Teesdale you should turn to page 27.

Crossing the fast-moving traffic of the A66 is a risky business. On the far side of the road and to the left of the house and barn of Pasture End the route heads uphill beside a wall, then bears north-east towards the bracken-covered slope of Ravock, before turning back north-west to make for a cairn and the ruins of a stone hut called Ravock Castle. The path is not always clear but once over the crest of the hill a straight wall on the far side of Deep Dale marks the route. There is a concrete footbridge over the whisky-coloured waters of Deepdale Beck.

Bowes Moor is at its best in August and September when the heather is in flower; May and June are enlivened by golden plovers and curlews, and some impressive insects including the emperor, fox and northern eggar moths. Regular burning of the heather is necessary to keep it fresh and green, sufficient to feed healthy populations of grouse and sheep.

At God's Bridge the River Greta disappears beneath the limestone.

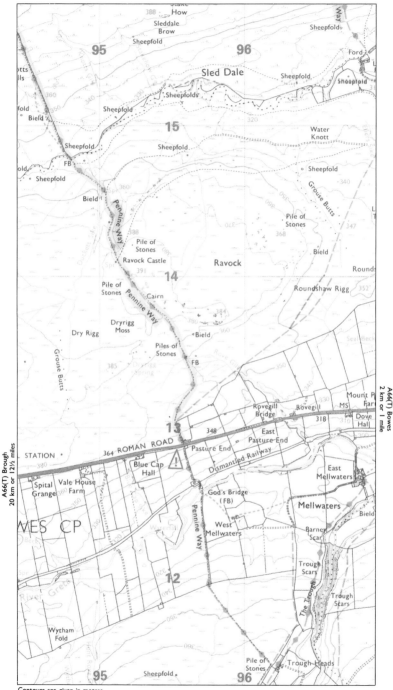

Contours are given in metres
The vertical interval is 10m

Once across Deep Dale the Way goes through a gate and follows a path beside a dry stone wall, climbing via several false crests to Race Yate Rigg. On this broad ridge the wall is left behind and Bowes Moor merges into Cotherstone Moor. In rain or mist this sweep of featureless waste is daunting and it is wise to use a compass, but in good visibility Baldersdale and its reservoirs are in sight and the route descends along a straight path across grassy or moss-covered moorland, keeping well left of Burners Hill to meet a road just south of Clove Lodge Farm.

At this point the alternative routes merge and this section is continued on page 31. If, however, you are starting out from Bowes itself, the next section describes the route from Bowes to Baldersdale.

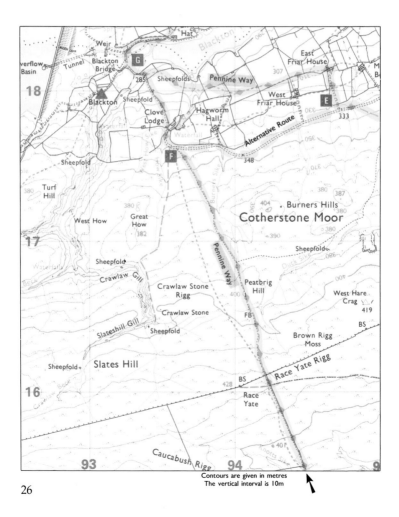

Contours are given in metres
The vertical interval is 10m

Bowes Castle, the ultimate defensive system of its day, was already a useless ruin 500 years ago.

Bowes has known busier days. The village occupies a strategic position on the Stainmore Gap; the Romans built a fort here to defend the road linking Watling Street at Penrith with Dere Street (the northern extension of Ermine Street) at Scotch Corner. The levelled site of the fort, called Lavatrae, was used again in the 12th century when a Norman keep was built on the spot **1**. Unfortunately this was squabbled over by everyone from kings and archbishops to terrorists and outlaws, and by the mid 14th century it was little more than a ruin – but such a substantial ruin that the immensely thick walls are still standing today.

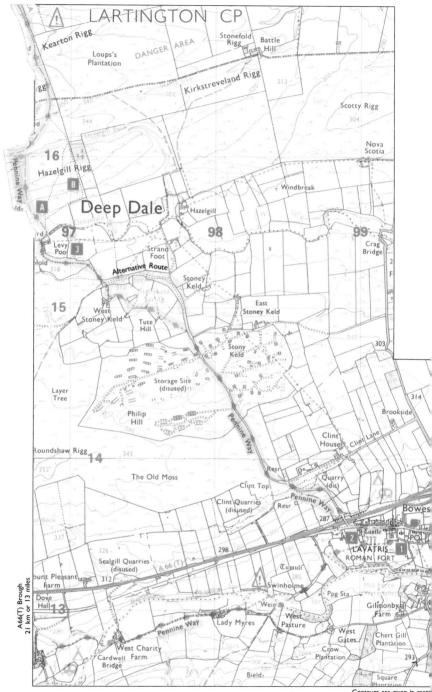

Contours are given in metr
The vertical interval is 10r

At the end of the main street, opposite West End Farm, there is an unusual square house 2, now a private dwelling but once a sort of transport café and originally a school managed by a gentleman called William Shaw. In January 1838 Charles Dickens came to stay at the nearby Unicorn Inn and was so impressed by William Shaw's Academy that he caricatured it as Dotheboys Hall in *Nicholas Nickleby*. Whether the place was quite so horrific as the one he portrayed is debatable but it is quite possible in the hard times of early Victorian England. William Shaw, the original Wackford Squeers, and George Ashton Taylor, who is supposed to have inspired the character Smike, are buried in the churchyard close by.

Under a slight cloud of Dickensian depression, the Way follows a tarmac road across the busy bypass (not shown on map) of the A66 trunk road and heads north-west uphill with rushy moorland on either side. Notices appear warning of the dangers of poisonous gas. Old Air Ministry buildings and storage sheds have been demolished but their foundations and floors remain, and the signs speed you on your way in a state of unutterable gloom. For once the abundance of redshanks, snipe, lapwings and curlews only compounds the feeling that you are in an unwholesome, unpeopled wilderness. Rather than bear left to Tute Hill along the official route it is a good idea to keep north along the road, past Stoney Keld and Strand Foot, then west, staying with the road until it reaches West Stoney Keld, at which the Way bears right (north-west) along a track and through a gate and into open pasture. Past a ruined barn a path bears west-north-west above Levy Pool, then drops down to pass close by the ruined farm. These moors have a high number of derelict steadings; hard work and poverty, and the lure of new industries, broke up the rural communities.

Levy Pool 3 has a fascinating roof, partly heather-thatched and partly stone-slabbed (see page 42). A muddy track leads through a gate below the ruined outbuildings. The Way crosses the Deepdale Beck via slippery stones and heads north across featureless rough terrain **A** over grassy ridges and across the marshy Hazelgill Beck, keeping to the right of an extensive mire before bearing north-east to a dry stone wall. Alternatively (and more sensibly) bear right after Deepdale Beck to pick up the wall earlier **B** and simply follow this northwards, past little alder groves, to meet a wall and a gate with the ruins of West Loups's to the east. The whole area to the east of the wall is Ministry of Defence land, with warning notices and red flags.

Once through the gate **C** (*see map on page 31, continuing below*) there are excellent views across a wide sweep of moorland. The Way takes a clear line, heading north-west and making for a point just to the right of the significant gritstone outcrop of Goldsborough **D**. This part of Cotherstone Moor has more character than Sled Dale but the route is still indistinct. A compass is essential. The moor is inhabited by Swaledale sheep but fewer moorland birds, and the vegetation is poor. Several rocks along the route bear cup and ring marks, complex patterns carved during the Bronze Age. Away to the right (north-east) the drainage runs to a gap at the headwater of Yawd Sike with views beyond of the Hamsterley Fells.

The Way continues west-north-west, below the hard face of Goldsborough, then angles northwards over the crest of the ridge to pick up a path north-west, down to Baldersdale and an unfenced road. At this road the official route turns left, then right along a drive **E** to East Friar Farm before heading westward to the end of Blackton Reservoir. This route is seldom used and it is a better idea to stay with the road which heads west-north-west below Burners Hills with the flat-topped and cairned hill of Shacklesborough in the far distance.

Just beyond Hagworm Hall the well-trodden path of the direct Pennine Way route from Keld leads out on to the road from the left **F**.

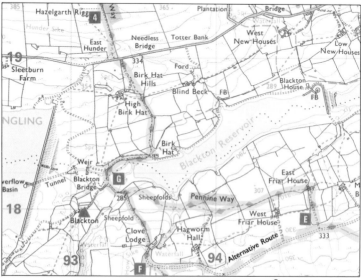

Contours are given in metres
The vertical interval is 10m

The Way arcs north along the road, and down to Clove Lodge. Through the gate it crosses the yard and bears left, then heads downhill to cross a little bridge with a meandering stream and the reservoir to the right; here all the possible routes are united. The Way heads north over the larger Blackton Bridge **G** with the grassed dam wall of Baldershead Reservoir to the left. The Baldersdale reservoirs, and those yet to be encountered in the Lune Valley to the north, gather the ample rainfall of Stainmore and were created to control the Tees and to slake the industrial thirst of Cleveland.

A path leads to the left (south-west) off the track at this point, heading for the youth hostel at Blackton. For those who have walked from Keld this is a likely stopover, the alternative being bed and breakfast in one of the farms or cottages in the valley.

From Blackton Bridge the Way climbs eastwards, above the shallow head of the reservoir, through Birk Hat where a path leads left (north) down to a step stile through a wall, then uphill through pastures and meadows. Past High Birk Hat the Way continues up to a road, turning left then right and uphill again over rushy pasture. Rushes are a sign of badly drained, impoverished ground, overstocked for too many years, but they give a warm orange glow lasting most of the winter and spring. On the brow of the hill **4** there are views ahead over Lunedale and Teesdale (to the north-east), and to the left over Hunderthwaite Moor, dominated in the foreground by Kelton Hill.

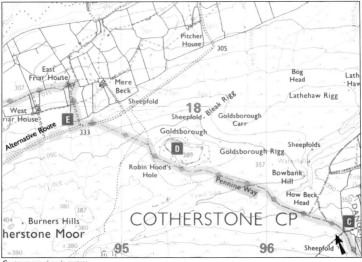

Contours are given in metres
The vertical interval is 10m

The Way now drops down into the Lune Valley, following a wall at first, then moving away from this to cross a stile at a gate in the bottom wall and making for the farm buildings of Beck Head. Below lie two reservoirs, the impressive dam wall and spillway of Selset to the left **5** and Grassholme to the right. Grassholme's marshy shallows, between Selset Weir and the side road to Grassholme Farm, are designated a nature reserve **6** and during the spring and summer a large colony of black-headed gulls make it a noisy and bustling place. There is a path diagonally across meadows towards the road at How. A sign asks walkers to keep in single file. This makes obvious sense in June when the hay crop is knee-high and flecked with flowers, but for much of the year the meadows are indistinguishable from pastures and are grazed by sheep or cattle.

At the road the Way used to bear right then sharp left around the converted farmstead, but no path exists now and it is necessary to walk further along the road until a crossroad is reached **H**, below the newly afforested slopes of Brownberry. Turn left (north-west) and walk down to cross the reservoir at a bridge, then climb the road to Grassholme Farm **I**. This is another diversion for the sake of the hay crop, through the farmyard and north along a clear path. The Way then leads uphill through a delightful patchwork of meadows, from barn to barn and eventually to a road. Directly across the road, a track leads to Wythes Hill Farm, at which the Way bears left and goes down a walled track, then across a stream and through a gate, and finally north-east and east over rough pasture towards a field barn **J**. The route is now indistinct but the going is easy.

From the barn the Way contours around Harter Fell. The views have changed; away to the south and south-west are the high fells of Yorkshire and Cumbria, but the middle distance is now dominated by a network of meadows and fertile pastures crowding Teesdale and Lunedale. Cutting the corner of the ridge, with the old workings of Greengates quarry to the right **7**, the Way stays on the middle contour of the hill and passes through several old walled pastures before dropping down along a well-marked grassy path, heading north-east towards the village of Middleton in Teesdale.

The knoll at the end of the ridge to the right (east) is Kirkcarrion **8**, a Bronze Age tumulus or burial site now planted with pines. It is visible for miles around, but is the sort of place that no footpath ever goes near. For centuries people have avoided it and children are afraid of seeing ghosts there.

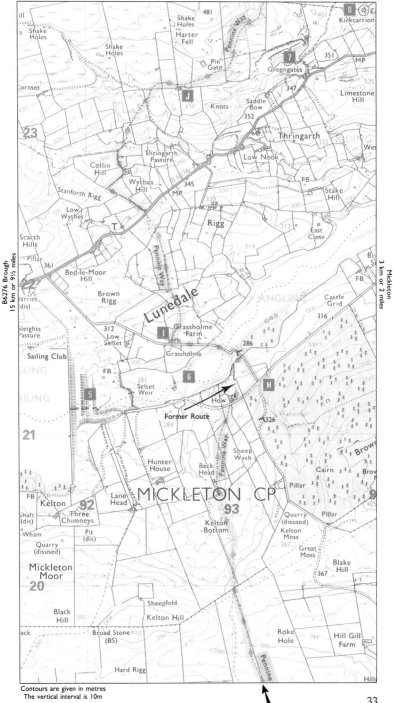

Contours are given in metres
The vertical interval is 10m

33

The cairned path heads down over rolling pasture to a gate in the field corner **K**, then continues more steeply to cross an old railway line, long dismantled, and emerge on a side road (*see map on page 35, continuing below*). The Way turns right then left along the main road, the B6277 north towards Middleton, but before the Tees bridge **L** it turns left along a track and leads through meadowland on the south bank of the Tees. For a while the path stays away from the river bank. To the north is the town, Middleton **9**, a Saxon settlement which expanded dramatically in the 18th century when the 'Quaker Company' – the London Lead Company – opened mines in the area. To the south beyond the river terrace lies the Whin Sill, a cliff of quartz-dolerite, and similar to basalt. This narrow ribbon of rock

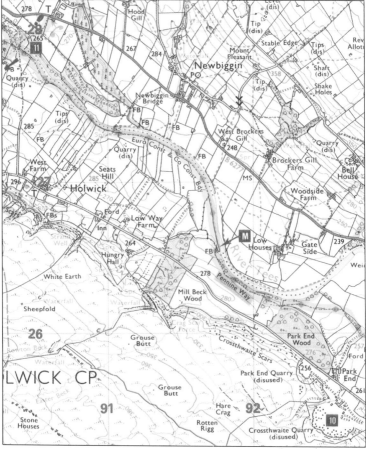

Contours are given in metres
The vertical interval is 10m

extends across northern England and forms some of the most impressive scenery of the Pennine Way. In many places the Whin Sill has been quarried for roadstone, and Crossthwaite **10** is the first of many cavities in the face of the Sill.

Where Rowton Beck meets the Tees **M**, east of Holwick, the Way at last drops down to the river bank and in summer the day becomes a gentle liaison with the river. Dippers, grey wagtails, common sandpipers and goosanders fly up and down, and the alder and sallow bushes are full of willow warblers, blackcaps and redstarts. Heavy rainfall, particularly in winter and spring, can make the liaison a deafening one-way tirade; the Tees is not as tame as it looks and it is best to treat it with respect.

Past Scoberry Bridge, and on to Wynch Bridge **11**, a little suspension bridge down from Bowlees on the B6277, the Way softens into a local beauty spot. The original Wynch Bridge was built in 1704 and was used by miners, but in 1820 it collapsed, killing one man. The present bridge was built in 1830.

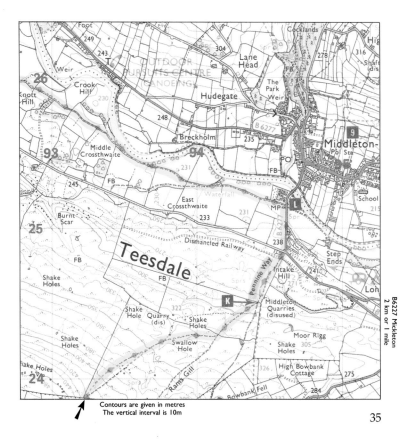

Contours are given in metres
The vertical interval is 10m

B6227 Mickleton
2 km or 1 mile

Rivers erode their beds until they reach harder rock, at which point they form steps or nick points. Whinstone is extremely hard and several famous waterfalls are to be found where the Sill outcrops. The first and least dramatic of these is Low Force **12**, a pretty place, ideal for a picnic, but uncomfortably popular. It is here that walkers begin to notice unusual flowers, the special plants that have given Teesdale its international reputation (see page 53). Globe flower is abundant, and the rocks have patches of both shrubby and alpine cinquefoil. Further on, just past Holwick Head Bridge, the Way climbs along a well-used path and enters the Teesdale National Nature Reserve at a stile **N**. Clearly, the number of people walking this route has made the Nature Conservancy Council take steps to minimise damage; the boardwalks detract from the pleasure of the walk but help to preserve the unique wildlife habitat. The first thing you notice about the path above Keedholm Scar **13** is that the bushes clothing the slopes grow either tall and thin or low and wide, but they are all junipers. Juniper wood, known as savin, was once used to make the best charcoal for use in the gunpowder industry, and the berries were harvested to flavour London gin. These days juniper is most often encountered in garden centres. In the middle of the dream-like experience of the ancient junipers you begin to hear a distant sound of thunder and soon a view of High Force **14** is framed between trees on the edge of the gorge. This is by far the best way to see this most famous of falls. On the far bank you have to pay and elbow your way past shoals of tourists; here you can pretend to be alone. High Force crashes from a shelf of dolerite over a horizontal band of shale to a deep dark plunge pool 69 feet (21 metres) below. The water is always brown and peaty, and very cold. Considering its stature, High Force is remarkably unspoilt; less so than many of the 'awesome' little Lakeland cataracts made famous by Wordsworth.

CIRCULAR WALK: UPPER TEESDALE AND CRONKLEY FELL
11½ miles (18.5 km) (see maps on pages 37–9)

This walk is a good introduction to Teesdale. Park in the lay-by at Bowlees and walk down to the Wynch Bridge, then follow the path uphill to contour westwards on the lower fell slopes. This leads quite steeply on to Cronkley Fell, then down to the River Tees which is then followed back to the Wynch Bridge.

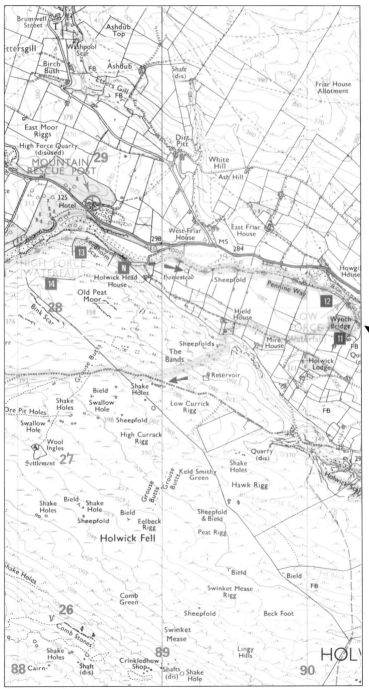

Contours are given in metres
The vertical interval is 10m

37

The path leads out of the woodland beside the top of the waterfall, then heads upstream (*see map on page 39*). The Tees subsides into a ribbon of blue water again; the thunder dies and is replaced by the call of sandpipers, oystercatchers and redshanks. On the north bank a sizeable slice of the hillside has been taken away by a quarry **15**. Beside this is Dine Holm Scar, which has tiers of heather and juniper. Bracken Rigg **16**, a mild climb, is free of bracken but also has an ageing crop of junipers, perhaps making you think wistfully of a gin and tonic. The word gin comes from the French for juniper, 'genevier'.

On the crest of the hill, where the scatter of trees opens out, there are good views of the fells to the south, of Cronkley, and the cairned summit of Noon Hill. The ridge of Bracken Rigg leads westwards and the Pennine Way takes this easy line down

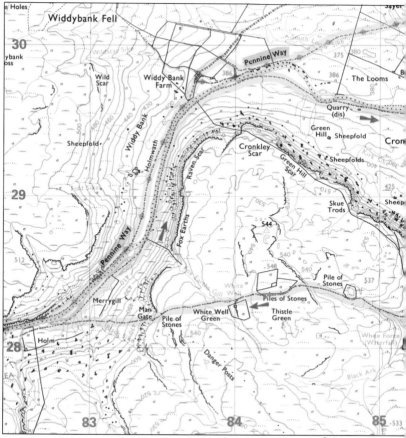

Contours are given in metre
The vertical interval is 10mi

towards a fence but bears right to meet a wall. The Way continues beside a wall to a stile, then down a gully and so to Cronkley Farm. From here a track heads north to a farm access bridge. It is now possible either to take a footpath **O** north-east to Forest-in-Teesdale or to head along the Way on the north bank of the Tees, past the confluence of Langdon Beck and turn right at the next footbridge up to the B6277 and the hamlet of Langdon Beck, where there is a youth hostel.

A long day, and not the most exhilarating of walks, but if it is early summer there will be ample recompense in the beauty of the flower-studded meadows and riverside pastures.

Contours are given in metres
The vertical interval is 10m

Above Wynch Bridge the Tees is at its most picturesque.

Levy Pool

Crumbling barns and cottages are a common sight on the Pennines. For many years the ruin of Levy Pool 3, near Bowes, attracted special attention from Pennine Way walkers because in younger days it had so clearly been a thriving and lively place. Children had been born and raised here, had grown up to farm and to raise farming families. Eventually times changed and the sons of Levy Pool sought their livelihoods elsewhere. The derelict farm buildings have recently been sold and planning permission has been granted for necessary alterations. What will the future hold? Will the house fall down or will it be lived in again? Whatever happens, Levy Pool will never be the same. Take your own photographs and compare them with the one opposite from 1916 and with the recent (1988) view of the ruins.

The steading of Levy Pool faces south, its back to the steep bank above Deepdale Beck. The main row of buildings comprises barn, farmhouse, cow-shed ('byre'), stalls, outhouse and cartshed. The farmhouse has perfectly square windows with solid sandstone sills and lintels, and the lintel above the inner door bears the date mark 1776. Originally all the roofs were thatched with heather, following a tradition dating back at least to medieval times, requiring a high gable with a steeply pitched roof to repel rain and snow. On some of the buildings sandstone flags or slates had replaced the 'black-thack' long before the steading reached the end of its working life. The roof of the byre has the only remaining thatch, and by the time this book is printed it may already have collapsed or been replaced. It was composed of bolted A-frames and sawn cross-beams. Rows of closely spaced rafters, mostly untrimmed trunks of young pine trees, were nailed to the ridge and supported on headstones at the eaves. A foot-thick blanket of heather completed the job.

Only a handful of heather-thatched farmhouses and cottages survive in England. All the natural building materials were readily available here at Levy Pool before the First World War, but there are now few living pines or heather bushes within sight of the farm. It was built to suit its setting and its time has now passed.

*(Above) Levy Pool and the Robinson family c. 1916. The hillside wood-land to the north-east is now reduced to a few skeletal pines.
(Below) Levy Pool in 1988.*

Forest-in-Teesdale to Dufton

13½ miles (21.7 km)

Saur Hill Bridge **A** is a good place from which to contemplate a day's walk, though this part of the Pennine Way has no obvious point to start (or finish if walking south) so the choice is arbitrary. The bridge spans Langdon Beck, wide and shallow and ever-changing. Grey and yellow wagtails hawk for flies along banks and dippers usually nest in the stonework below. Signs by the gate in the middle of the bridge inform you that it is 121 miles (195 km) to Kirk Yetholm and 149 miles (240 km) to Edale; these measurements follow Wainwright and add up to 270 miles (435 km), which is his total estimate for the walking distance of the Pennine Way.

From the bridge the Way follows a track to Saur Hill Farm ('Sayer Hill' on the map) but angles up to the left in front of the farm and continues along an ill-defined path across meadowland and over a step-stile, and so across pastures and past a national nature reserve sign, making for the gap to the north (right) of Cronkley Fell. The River Tees is heard before it is seen, a conversational jumble of sounds accompanied in summer by piping sandpipers, which nest on the gravels, and redshank, which nest among the marsh grasses.

The Way has hardly settled beside the river before it is diverted to the right, over a stile and on to a track **B**, and through Widdy Bank Farm **17**. The little farm, like most of its neighbours on the north side of the river, is part of the Raby estate reputed to stretch most of the way to Darlington. The original shell of the farmhouse dates back to 1698; hundreds of coats of whitewash help to keep the walls wind- and weatherproof. The application of whitewash is part of the lease agreement – hence all the white farm buildings in Teesdale. The farm extends to 2,000 acres (809 hectares) mostly of very rough grazing with just 30 acres (12 hectares) of hay, so most winter feed has to be bought in as silage. A few cattle graze the inby fields close to the farms but the fells are wild and are the territory of hardy Swaledale sheep.

Part of the route keeps to the track, close beside the Tees. For centuries the river marked the boundary between the North Riding of Yorkshire and County Durham. Now the county line lies further south but the two sides of the dale lie in separate ownership (the land south of the river is part of the Earl of

Strathmore's estate) and so have different traditions, reflected in every farmhouse and field.

The Tees snakes its way between high fells composed of sedimentary rock (the typical cycle of limestone-shale-sandstone) but influenced by fire. Silurian slate, 500 million years old, underlies the Carboniferous sediments; soft green slate was once quarried nearby and made into pencils. The word 'widdy', as in Widdy Bank, was a local name for the slate pencils of Victorian classrooms. However, the most important geological event occurred less than 300 million years ago, when violent earthquakes forced molten rock between existing sediments. The rock itself cooled to form quartz-dolerite, exposed in Teesdale as the Whin Sill. Minerals were deposited in the faults, creating a stockpile of metal ores, and limestone was hardened and fractured into granules which outcropped as beds of 'sugar limestone' and were later colonised by arctic-alpine flowers (see page 53). Thus, whether visitors come to Teesdale for the views, the industrial history or the wildlife, the key lies in a single fiery episode at the end of the Carboniferous period.

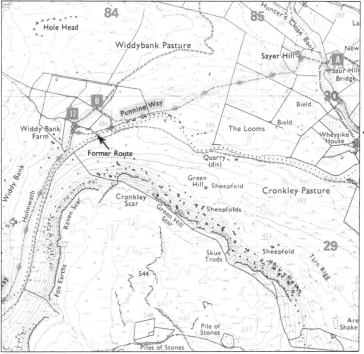

Contours are given in metres
The vertical interval is 10m

The path is easy to follow but difficult underfoot. Scree and boulder-fields alternate with duckboarding, making walking hazardous. Any spare attention should go to the steep rocky slopes and cliffs (or 'clints') to the right **18**, but few stops along the way may pay dividends.

This is a good place to look for ring ouzels, which are unusually common here. They may be closely related to blackbirds but are very shy and inclined to fly away rather than sit and display their white crescent-mark. An elusive soot-coloured thrush among the rowan bushes and whinstone boulders may well turn out to be a ring ouzel – especially if it goes 'peeoo' rather than 'pink pink'. However, when scared or close to its nest the ouzel goes 'teck teck', just like a black-bird.

Falcon Clints **19** are impressive, the hard whinstone geometry mellowed by green dabs of ferns and map lichen. Kestrels are often in evidence; other falcons (such as peregrines and merlins) are possible, but they are generally less inclined to show them-selves.

The Pennine Way stays close to the foot of the clints, turning north with the Tees opposite the confluence of the Maize Beck **C**. The path leads beside grassy river verges or scrambles its way over tumbled columns of dolerite, like the fallen ruins of a Greek temple. Years of wear by the feet of tourists have polished the boulders along the path and made them a hazard in wet weather. Twisted ankles and broken hips are regular mishaps on this section.

The noise of angry water has by now ushered in another waterfall. From this approach Cauldron Snout **20** is an explosive torrent, a broad fan of white spray escaping from a narrow cleft in the Whin Sill. The stone buttresses on the shoulders of the waterfall are a convenient place to stop for a lunch break. Take the opportunity to enjoy the vision of an untamed Tees; at the top of the rock climb lies the dam wall of Cow Green Reservoir **21**. The reservoir was the subject of a public inquiry during the 1960s.

The Tees is crossed, and Cumbria entered, by meeting a metalled track and following this westward **D**. The Way stays with the track as it heads south-west to Birkdale. There are good views back along the upper Tees and over Cronkley Fell, and south to Mickle Fell which rises to 2,585 feet (788 metres). Birkdale **E**, which is a mountain rescue sub-post, is approached by keeping to the tarmac and going through the farmyard, after

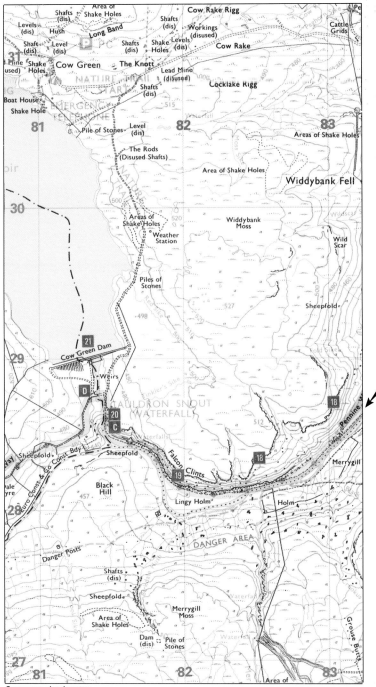

Contours are given in metres
The vertical interval is 10m

which the track is replaced by a grassy path (*see map on page 49, continuing below*). Once across the Grain Beck **F** the whole atmosphere of the walk changes. East is giving way to west; even the sheep are from Dufton, where the farms have fell grazing rights as far as Cow Green.

A boggy uphill slog leads to a cairn by the old mine spoil of Moss Shop **22**. 'Shop' was the name given to very basic bunkhouse accommodation provided for miners on the fells; at weekends they returned to their homes. The indistinct path then leads onwards, past posts and cairns, to a featureless horizon. The brow of the hill slope is grassy and cairned. Mickle Fell lies across the Maize Beck to the left (south-east), Meldon Hill rises 2,487 feet (758 metres) to the right (north-north-west).

The Way heads west-south-west along an indistinct path with few cairns; the orientation is best achieved by keeping parallel with Ministry of Defence signs, then dropping obliquely downhill across tussocky grass and deep sikes, or small streams, to meet the Maize Beck **G**. The landscape is bleak and

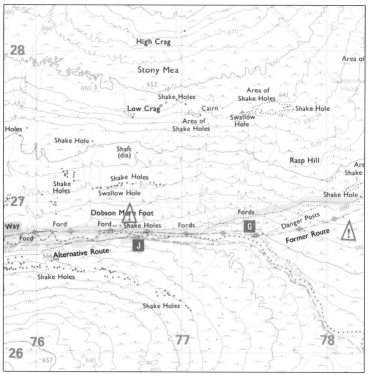

Contours are given in metres
The vertical interval is 10m

treeless – there are no dwellings in sight, and no sounds to be heard except for the calls of larks and pipits, curlews and golden plovers.

After travelling through such a lonely land the Maize Beck is a welcome relief. The walk along its north bank, beside shelves of limestone colonised by pearlwort and thyme, is idyllic but brief. A choice has to be made now concerning the approach to High Cup, the most impressive feature on the northern stretch of the Pennine Way. If the beck is running high it is best to keep to its north bank, bearing north to cross it at a footbridge over a limestone gorge **H**, then heading south-west to the edge of High Cup **I**. But in good weather, when Maize Beck is at its most lovely, it can be forded beyond a waymarked sign **J**, from where a path slants uphill on the flank of Murton Fell. If there is any real doubt, or if the stones look too slippery, keep to the safe route. By crossing the beck and heading west-south-west up the

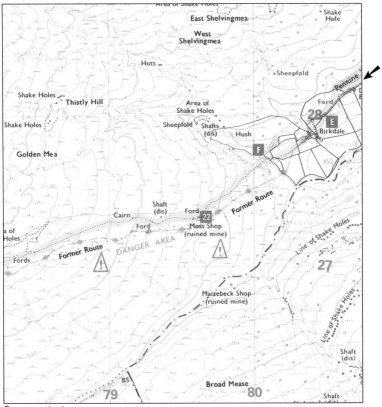

Contours are given in metres
The vertical interval is 10m

clear path to High Cup Plain it is possible to approach the head of the valley at the nick of High Cup Gill and so find yourself at the pivotal point of the whole landscape **K** (*see map on page 51, continuing below*). The world suddenly opens out beneath you. A curtain of sheer whinstone cliffs sweeps left and right, beneath which cascades of grass and scree curve inwards to create a deep basin. The effect is stunning; although on a lesser scale, the sensation is akin to standing on the edge of the Rift Valley. Ravens and peregrines patrol the grey columns of dolerite. At the foot of the amphitheatre, High Cup Gill **23**, like a fine silver thread stitched into rugged tweed, traces its way south-west to the Eden Valley. Beyond lie the Lakeland fells.

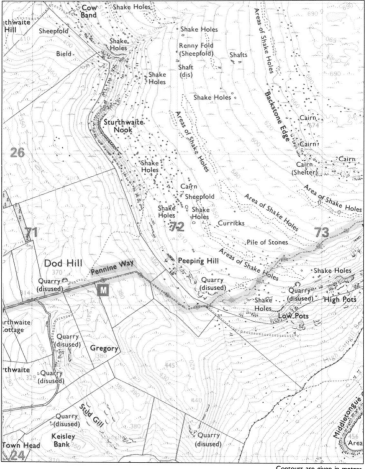

Contours are given in metres
The vertical interval is 10m

A path bears right, at first close to the edge of the precipice but soon along a safe grassy bank, heading south-west above a stack of rock called Nichol Chair **L**. In good visibility the far wall of High Cup seems close enough to touch, but it is getting further away by the minute as the widening valley opens out to Middletongue Crag. The Pennines melt away; all that remains is the descent into the Vale of Eden.

Cairns mark the rocky downhill path. To lose the Pennines at this point is galling; north of Dufton the Way has to regain all this height and more. A puzzled walker might look at the map and ask why there is no route straight across to Knock Fell. But Dufton provides the only possible overnight stop. There is no path across the treacherous fells to cut the corner, and in any case it is a long way to Garrigill.

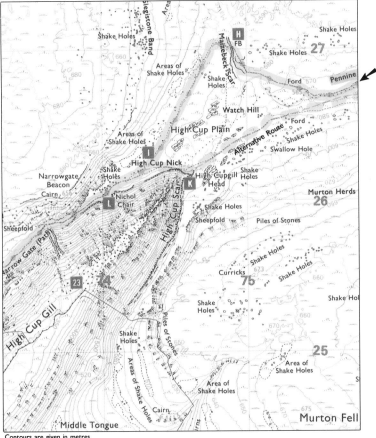

Contours are given in metres
The vertical interval is 10m

The path drops down to a drove road **M** which leads directly to Dufton **24**. Green rolling pastures, cobwebbed by dry stone walls, appear on either side, and hedgerows of blackthorn and gooseberry soften the roadside as it reaches Town Head **N**. Here, the Way turns right along the main road into the village, past small farms and brightly coloured cottages. Dufton is a picturesque interlude. All necessary facilities and services are available. It is possible to sit on the village green **O** outside the post office, pub or youth hostel and see where you have come from or where you are going to. The Way could not be better served.

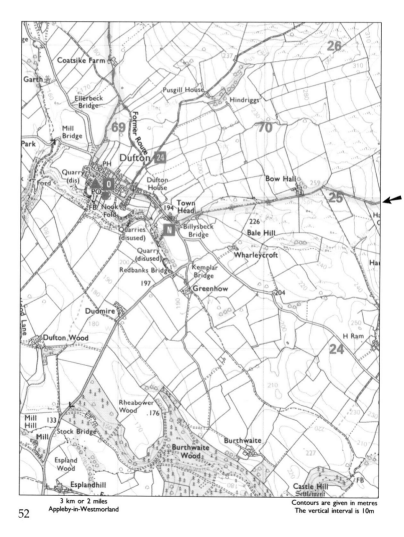

3 km or 2 miles
Appleby-in-Westmorland

Contours are given in metres
The vertical interval is 10m

The Teesdale rarities

Anyone with a knowledge of wild flowers will have heard of Upper Teesdale, particularly since the late 1960s when a public inquiry was held to consider the case against flooding part of the famous Widdybank Fell to form Cow Green Reservoir. Eventually Parliament approved the reservoir scheme and the valley was flooded in 1971–2 but the flowers still remain on the adjacent fells, a little rarer, a little more restricted in their range.

For many years no one could explain why such places as Teesdale and Ben Lawers in Scotland seemed to have more than their share of special flowers, but in 1949 Sir Harry Godwin suggested they were fragments of a carpet of tundra vegetation which had covered most of Britain after the Ice Age but had then been shaded out by trees when the climate improved. One of Teesdale's great rarities, the dwarf birch, occurs in one small patch and radiocarbon dating of leaf and pollen remains in the peat underneath it has provided a continuous inch-by-inch record stretching back 10,000 years. Thus it appears that Teesdale was a grassy island in a sea of forest, and its plants have been able to cope with the belated arrival of farming and any subsequent changes in the climate.

The living history of the landscape is impressive but in practice much of Teesdale looks unremarkable and its commonest plants are those found everywhere. Daisies and dandelions, and a host of other weeds, probably arrived as seeds on animals' hoofs or walkers' boots. The dominant communities of the unimproved pasture include tormentil and heath bedstraw, as they do on most other stretches of the Pennine Way. However, the close combination of primary habitats, marsh and bog, riverside, scree, upland heath and limestone grassland make this one of the best places to stop for a few minutes to see the flowers of the uplands.

The most unusual habitat is the 'sugar limestone' found on Widdybank and Cronkley Fells. When the Whin Sill was created, from molten rock pushed up through the earth's crust nearly 300 million years ago, the strata next to the hot rock was metamorphosed, and in the case of the existing limestone a crumbly sort of marble was the result. The Pennine Way does not lead across the plateaux on which most of this sugar limestone is found, but there are outcrops or shelves on several of the slopes and it is possible to find most of the lime-loving plants by following the becks radiating away from the main valley.

The footpath south-west from the B6277, near Langdon Beck Youth Hostel, to

Saur Hill Bridge. In spring marsh marigold flowers abound.

The most famous Teesdale plant is the spring gentian, a low-growing and short-lived perennial which produces a large, five-petalled flower, a vivid and unforgettable blue in colour. The flowers open only on bright sunny days and the season is short and variable. Sometimes the plant is in seed by the end of May, sometimes it is still out at the end of June. Sometimes the flowers are prolific, at other times they are sparse. Unpredictability added to rarity (Western Ireland is the only other British locality) make the spring gentian an aristocrat.

By contrast, the Teesdale violet is a rather untidy little plant despite its rarity. It grows on broken limey ground, especially where there are lots of molehills, and is smaller and more pink than other violets. Often Teesdale violets grow alongside bird's eye primrose and suffer by comparison; the pastel shades and

The intense blue of the spring gentian is legendary; so is its rarity.

Bird's eye primrose is a speciality of the North Yorks Pennines.

neat structure of the pink-flowered primrose make it one of the prettiest of plants, less gaudy than the gentian, more finely formed than the violet. These three plants probably symbolise Teesdale's flora to most people.

At the right time of year a walk through Teesdale on the Pennine Way should produce shrubby cinquefoil, globeflower, wood cranesbill, yellow and meadow saxifrage and a host of other local plants. The real rarities, such as alpine forget-me-not, mountain avens, bitter milkwort, alpine bartsia and bog sandwort, are not so easy to find and often occur in restricted localities on the fell tops. Teesdale is a national nature reserve and random trampling is frowned on. It would be a tragedy if a plant had managed to survive for more than 10,000 years only to be exterminated by a misplaced boot.

Dufton
to Alston

19½ miles (31.4 km)

In poor weather the North Pennines can test the heart of any walker, and avoiding poor weather requires luck rather than judgement. The headwaters of the Tees lattice a windswept plateau of moorland, rising in the west to a chain of mighty hills. This section of the Way begins in the verdant valley of the River Eden, then climbs sharply to Knock Fell and heads north-west to link the summits of Dun Fell and Cross Fell, before arcing north-east over open moors and commons to reach the South Tyne at Garrigill, and thence along the river to Alston. A long day, strenuous at first but earning the reward of incomparable views. Few other sections of the trail cast so potent a spell.

Dufton was a lead-mining village, yet it lacks the hard edge of Alston or Middleton and is built around a tree-lined green. The older houses are of warm red sandstone or whitewash; new houses are pebble-dashed. Garden gates are overhung by rose and honeysuckle and the walls are part-hidden by clumps of toadflax and corydalis. At first sight, Dufton has an enviable air of prosperity and seems more West Country than Westmorland. The Pennine Way leaves the main road close to the Methodist church **A**, beside Dufton Hall and a converted cottage bearing the inscription LWONIN FYEAT 1648. The words may look Welsh but are actually local dialect for Lane (or Lonnen) Foot. The original route heads north-east along a track, then north-west along a path, but a stream has made this impassable and an alternative is signed which runs along a back lane behind Dufton Hall Farm.

The muddy back lane presents a very different face of the village, battened down against the Helm Wind. This fierce and infamous blast is caused when an easterly airflow rushes downhill to meet the warm air mass of the Eden Valley; the 'helm' refers to an associated helmet or pall of cloud hanging over Cross Fell.

At the western end of the village the alternative route turns right along the road and heads downhill, then bears right **B** along a track signed 'Pennine Way via Great Dun Fell'. This leads back on to the official route along a hawthorn-lined track, past Coatsike Farm **C**. The track resolves itself into an ancient sunken way called Hurning Lane, lined with thorn and ash

Dufton Hall Farm in Cumbria.

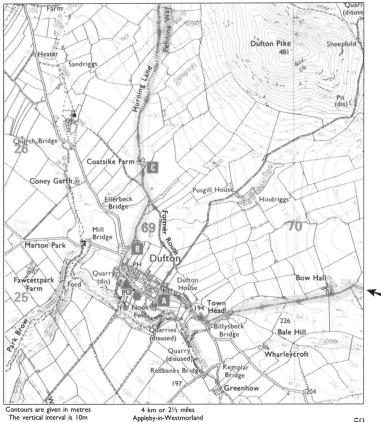

Contours are given in metres
The vertical interval is 10m

4 km or 2½ miles
Appleby-in-Westmorland

trees. Ash was widely planted in previous centuries because it was so useful – it was palatable to hungry stock and the wood could be worked into tool handles or used as a domestic fuel.

It is much easier to walk beside this forgotten byway than along it; no string of pack ponies has followed this road for generations and it is overhung with clutching branches. There is an air of haunted neglect about the place. Halsteads **D**, the next farm along, is deserted and has a similar bitter-sweet atmosphere. Beyond this the Way contours around Cosca Hill, from where there is a wonderful view back across the Eden Valley to the Lakeland fells.

Great Rundale Beck is crossed at an old clapper bridge **25**, the stone slabs worn smooth by the comings and goings of shepherds, miners and long-distance walkers.

The whole character of the terrain now begins to change on the gradual ascent north-east towards the high fells. The gentle lowlands are left behind and rough pasture and moorland appear to the right and left. Curlews call, snipe drum and buzzards soar overhead – if you are lucky. Away to the left (north-west) is Knock Pike **26** which, like Dufton Pike, is remarkably green and looks out of character against the Pennine backdrop. In fact these conical hills have more in common with the northern Lake District; they are composed of Skiddaw slate and stand aloof from the Cross Fell range.

The old clapper bridge over Great Rundale Beck.

The security of the track is soon left behind on the lower slopes of Scald Fell; the Way bears left **E**, continuing north as the track turns east. Ahead are Cross Fell and Great Dun Fell – the latter all too obvious because of the radar installation on its summit. The high fells still look, and are, some distance away, but are getting nearer.

After crossing a footbridge over boulder-strewn Swindale Beck, the Way begins a much sharper climb and takes a direct line north-east along an indistinct but cairned path **F**, parallel to an impressively steep-sided chasm carrying the upper reaches of the beck.

The next 1¼ miles (2 km) are of steady ascent, the terrain sometimes boggy but generally good underfoot. Reference to a map reveals a jumble of words such as shake hole, hush, cairn and currick. On the ground these features are less distinct. 'Shake holes' are conical depressions caused by underground subsidence and erosion of limestone. 'Hushes' are gashes in hillsides caused by mining activity; dams were constructed across natural clefts and the water released to scour the vegetation from the fellside and expose mineral deposits. The

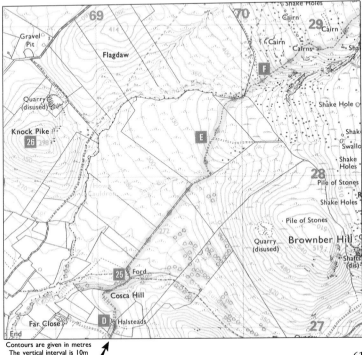

Contours are given in metres
The vertical interval is 10m

word 'cairn', now universally used to describe a pile of stones used as a waymark for walkers, used to refer to a mound of stones over an ancient burial site, while 'currick' was used for a pile of stones intended as a shepherd's viewpoint.

The long climb from cairn to cairn leads inexorably to Knock Old Man **27**, a great square obelisk of stones on the brow of Knock Fell overlooking the Eden Valley. The cairn provides some shelter from prevailing wind and rain (sunshine is unlikely to be a problem), but the top of the fell beckons and it is easy to push on, still heading north-east, to the summit cairn.

From here the Way changes direction and begins a north-west tack to link the major Pennine peaks. From the multi-cairned crown of Knock Fell **G** the route traverses rocky domes and drops down towards a road, with Great Dun Fell straight ahead. The small enclosure **28** marks a vegetation experiment undertaken by the Nature Conservancy Council; from Swindale Beck in the south to the Tees in the north, and from Cow Green in the east to Hanging Shaw in the west, stretches Moor House National Nature Reserve, an apparently barren wilderness notable for its birds of prey and arctic flowers. To the right of the path (north-east) lies a peaty plateau channelling water into the Trout Beck, which joins the Tees below the dwelling of Moor House. To the left **29** is one of several deep clefts in the Pennine ridge with exposed faces of limestone and whinstone.

At the tarmac road **H** the Way bears right and follows the road northwards until it reaches the entrance to the radar installation topping Great Dun Fell. Much has been written about this feature **30**. Its present manifestation is a white golf-ball with associated masts and buildings. It is easy to dwell on its negative aspects, which are inescapable. On the positive side, no one will ever get lost trying to find Great Dun Fell in anything short of white-out conditions. Also, aviation is safer for its presence.

It is possible to follow the road up to the fell top but this is far from direct. Conversely, the straight ascent is barred by the near-vertical trench of Dunfell Hush **31**. The official Pennine Way **I** bears right (north-east) along a track, then crosses the hush before bearing west, uphill to the radar station. This has two drawbacks. Snow often lies in the hush to an indeterminable depth, and there is no visible path uphill. The alternative **J** is to bear north-west, splitting the angle between the road and the track, heading for the left edge of the radar station and above the head of the hush. Either way, aim to reach the summit of Great Dun Fell to the right (east) of the radar station.

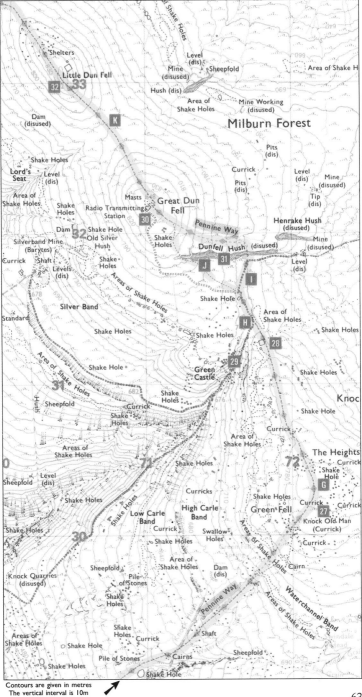

Contours are given in metres
The vertical interval is 10m

Cross Fell still dominates the northern skyline, but Little Dun Fell **32** is now visible in the foreground, an imposing and clear-cut land-form more significant than it looks on a map and irresistible to any ridge walker. The Way heads directly for it, sweeping downhill to a marshy saddle **K**, then climbing smartly to the open summit.

From Little Dun Fell the view back is disappointing but this is more than compensated for by the prospect of Cross Fell, which now takes on goliath proportions. It is the highest point on the Pennines, and from here it looks it. From the scatter of boulders on the collar of Little Dun Fell's summit, the Way drops directly again to another saddle or link in the chain. A drop of rain falling here may flow either east or west – east to Tees Head **33** and the catchment of the Tees and so to the North Sea at Middlesbrough, west to the Crowdundle Beck and via the Eden and Solway to the Irish Sea.

Peat hags and black puddles make the crossing of the headwaters unpleasant. The acidic flushes around Cross Fell boast several interesting but obscure plants. One of these is the alpine foxtail grass which has the distinction of being found in only a few places in northern Britain and nowhere else in Europe. The nearest neighbouring locality is Greenland. Limestone crags in these fells harbour more showy plants, such as roseroot and mossy saxifrage.

After negotiating the hags, the Way climbs steadily up a braided and boggy path **L**, heading straight up to the summit plateau rather than obliquely left as indicated on most maps. For several months each year fields of snow have to be traversed, and breasting the steep ice-shattered screes to reach the tall cairns on the edge of Cross Fell's table-top **M** is like stepping back into post-glacial Britain.

The surface of the plateau is stony and covered with short grass. *The Gentleman's Magazine* of 1747 describes the place as having 'a venerable aspect from the moss . . . and this can hardly draw a subsistence . . . so inconceivably barren is this distinguished eminence'. In many ways the summit resembles the Cairngorms and like this Scottish wilderness it is sometimes visited by mountain birds such as the dotterel.

Cross Fell triangulation point **34** stands at a height of 2,930 feet (893 metres). Nearby is a cross-shaped wind shelter which is remarkably effective in providing a temporary respite. Although it may have taken two-thirds of the day to get one-third of the distance, the remainder of the section is easy and a few minutes rest and contemplation are in order. On a clear day the distant views are impressive, but such days are unusual; in the words of the 1747 magazine, Cross Fell is 'generally ten months buried in snow and eleven in clouds'. It can be an evil place and was known as 'Fiend's Fell' until recent times. Christians may have tamed the title but the landscape is still pagan.

From the shelter the Way heads north-north-west from cairn to cairn, and descends via Crossfell Well towards a well-worn track **N**. The views to the north, over the headwaters of the

Contours are given in metres
The vertical interval is 10m

The Cross Fell plateau, looking south-east from the so-called 'Corpse Road'.

Black Burn, are wonderfully bleak. Once there would have been lead mines to catch the eye; now a sea of open moorland drifts to the far horizon with hardly a point of focus. The Way turns right to follow the track **35** – a very old Pennine crossing linking Garrigill with Kirkland, reputed (on rather flimsy evidence) to have been used to transport bodies for burial. This 'Corpse Road' provides an excellent, though hard, walking surface and the Way takes full advantage of it. After heading east-north-east beneath the impressive sweep of Cross Fell's north face, and past Greg's Hut **36** – an emergency overnight shelter with very basic facilities – the track turns north-north-east. The Way keeps with this all the way to Garrigill. Moorland lies all around. Sometimes the track passes old mine workings and its surface is strewn with 'gangue' – waste materials which include fluorspar. Pebbles or chips of fluorspar glow deep purple when wet, but they dry pale and opaque. Here and there pieces of galena (lead ore) can be picked up. These make good souvenirs but seem to get heavier and heavier through the day.

The walk along the Corpse Road continues for several miles. In general there are few remarkable features, merely a gradual increase in heather as the old mine workings and rough sheep walks give way to grouse moorland. Through a gate **O** the Way

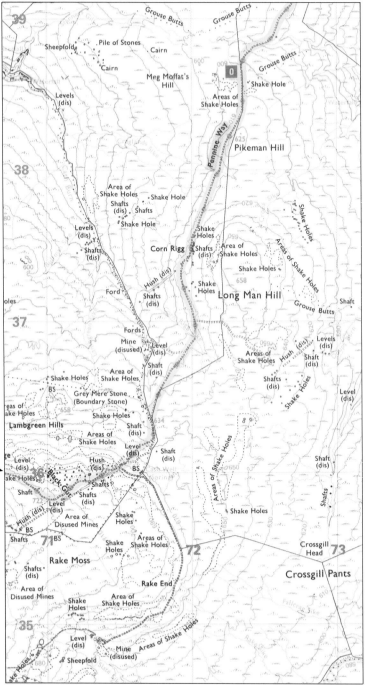

Contours are given in metres
The vertical interval is 10m

bears right then drops downhill to meet a wall **P**. The official route continues along the track, with the wall on the right, but soon turns right, through a gate **Q** and heads obliquely downhill. This path is rarely followed and the conventional route is to follow the track northwards through another gate **R** then, with walls on either side, to keep to this drove road as it descends steeply past a Methodist chapel **S** and left along the road into Garrigill.

The little village of Garrigill **37** (the name is derived from Gerard's Gill – gill being an old Norse word for a narrow valley) is clustered around a village green, but it has little else in common with Dufton; it stands in a cleft forged by the South Tyne River and its traditions are of the North-East.

The Way heads north-west along the main street but once out of the village, where the road bears uphill to the left, a stile **T** leads right and parallel to the river. After a poor start – the South Tyne suffers from a surfeit of rubbish dumps and old spoil heaps – this riverside walk is attractive and full of interest, but at the end of an upland walk it is difficult to adjust your senses and appreciate the scent of ramsons in the alder groves or the piping calls of oystercatchers and sandpipers along the river gravels.

Garrigill is an interesting little village, well worth a pause.

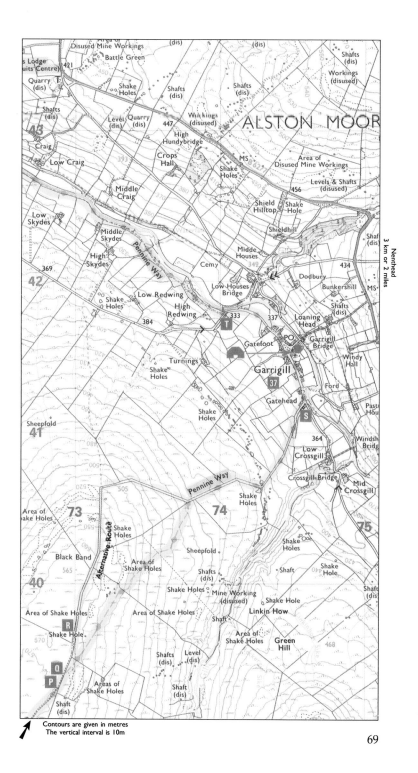

Eventually the Way crosses the river at a footbridge **U** and continues along the north bank, but after a step-stile by a gate **V** it bears right, obliquely uphill to Bleagate **W**. It then follows a line well above the river, mostly over pasture, along a well-signed and stiled path. If it is evening the sun will be setting over the high ridge linking Black Fell and Grey Nag in the west. The hills may seem to go on for ever, but this trackless wilderness, from Hartside to Cold Fell, is the reprise of the Pennines and what lies further north is the Whin Sill and the Cheviots.

The walk into Alston is completed along a firm, well-trodden path above a steep tree-shaded bank – a local beauty spot called the Firs **38**. Meeting dog-walkers and courting couples forces a rapid acclimatisation; it is you, not they, who have landed from outer space.

Alston

The little market town of Alston **39** wears a workaday face. Anyone driving across the Pennines from Hexham to Penrith, taking in the fine views along the A686, will be aware of a prosaic interlude of workshops and garages rather than the main town uphill to the east. The Pennine Way also does the town a disservice by sidestepping it and keeping to the South Tyne; it is only after several hundred yards that a view east over the river suggests there is more to the place than a shop-stop or bed and breakfast opportunity.

Alston is built close to the confluence of the Nent and the South Tyne. Houses, churches, schools and shops jostle for space on the rising ground. Although there are obvious signs of recent expansion, the core of the town is intact; on a bright sunny day Alston has the air of a hilltop village in Andalusia or Catalonia and should be explored in the same relaxed way. Even on the other 364 days, of icy winds or misty drizzle, it is worth walking up the cobbled main street from Town Foot, detouring past the Market Cross to the Butts or around Back o' the Burn to Town Head. Most of the buildings have a history but there has been little effort over the years to make them picturesque. Cars and vans are parked at random, anywhere and everywhere, and there always seem to be signs and hoardings on the pavements warning of roadworks or advertising fish and chips.

Alston is disarmingly honest about itself. It seems at first glance to be based around the needs of the local farming

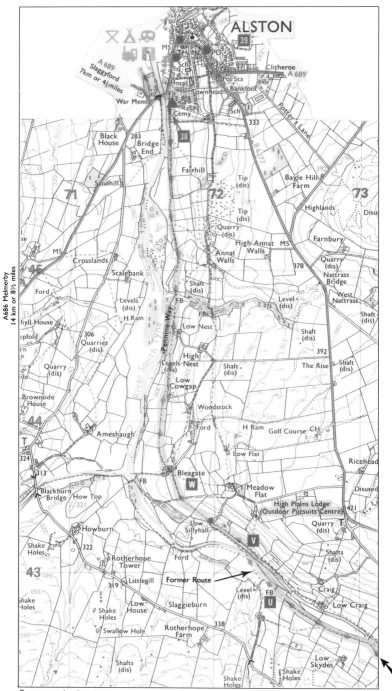

Contours are given in metres
The vertical interval is 10m

Alston is a town full of fascinating little shops.

community, and is reputed to be the highest market town in England (Buxton in Derbyshire shares the claim). In fact its roots go very much deeper, into the hills where silver was mined at least into medieval times and lead became a pervasive industry in the 18th and 19th centuries.

Alston was part of a royal estate leased to the king of Scotland in the 12th century but then held by the canons of Hexham Abbey until the Dissolution of the monasteries in the 16th century. For some years the developing village belonged to the Radcliffe family who lived at Dilston Hall a few miles east of Hexham. Some of the oldest surviving buildings, both manor houses and cottages, were built at this time and several carry 17th century date marks. The older town terraces have stone steps leading to a first-floor doorway. When the town began to expand the houses were easily split into sub-units with their own entrances. Thus Alston became a bustling little settlement of tall square houses, with a wide cobbled market place where people could meet and barter, bet, bait or brawl. The Butts, an area of alleyways behind St Augustine's Church, was used for archery when long-bow practice was compulsory, before the reign of Henry VIII. Nearby, just down from the church, stands the Angel Inn which dates back to 1614.

The Radcliffe connection came to a disastrous end when James Radcliffe, third Earl of Derwentwater and the illegitimate son of Charles II, joined James Stuart in the 1715 Rebellion. He was captured after the Battle of Preston and was executed in 1716. His brother Charles suffered a similar fate after the 1745 Rebellion. Alston became part of the Greenwich Hospital Estate and its associated mines were leased to the London Lead Company. When Dilston Hall was demolished, its clock and bell were given to the town; the workings have recently been restored and can be seen in St Augustine's Church. The hands are original but the face is a cunning fibreglass replica!

Most of present-day Alston town centre was built around 1800 when lead mining was flourishing. During the 19th century the place seemed to have a golden future. A short walk through the main streets at that time would have passed the Low Market and the busy High Market in front of the Crown Hotel; a slaughterhouse, a Wesleyan chapel and a Quaker meeting house, a grammar school, and a forge powered by a 14-foot overshot waterwheel. At the bottom of the town, on the road to Hexham, a railway station was opened in 1828 after plans for a narrow-gauge line had been approved by George Stephenson. Everything, except perhaps the climate, seemed to be set fair. Unfortunately the lead industry floundered in a few short years and Alston was stunned into a long and painful silence. Agriculture has kept the town going – just. Today there are signs of a revival and it is fascinating to see how the original mills and chapels have been transformed into engineering works, private dwellings, gift shops and galleries. However, because there has been no clear trend or development since the turn of the century, and no major rebuilding within the old heart of the town, there are much clearer links with the past. There are still rusting enamel signs advertising Oxo and the *Daily Telegraph*. One of the shops manages to combine selling old glass bottles and lamps with fresh fruit and vegetables. Half close your eyes and the delivery vans and cars could be wagons and pack ponies; the farmers and storekeepers talk in much the same way as they ever did. Conversely, with a few coats of paint, brushed-up stone work and appropriate street furniture, the market place could grace the cover of a holiday brochure.

The abiding charm of Alston lies in the fact that it has not quite become a tourist town. Certainly, the climate is against it. It lies in the heart of a cold land and its future, like its past, is tied to the Pennines.

Alston from the Pennine Way above the west bank of the South Tyne.

Alston to Greenhead

16½ miles (26.6 km)

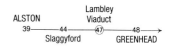
Some days are roses, others are thorns. If there is a disappointment on any section of the Pennine Way it is likely to be the long walk from Alston through Slaggyford and by Lambley to Greenhead. The sections to the south and north, the high Pennine Fells and Hadrian's Wall respectively, are spectacular. This linking section has few highlights other than the Roman associations of the Maiden Way and the great wilderness of Blenkinsopp Common.

Alston **39** rarely seems to get up early and the chances are that you will be crossing the A686 road bridge **A** well before anything is stirring at the market end of town. This encourages a smug satisfaction, soon to be dashed as you get into the country and see shepherds returning from the fells for breakfast.

The Pennine Way is signposted just after a right turn **B** where the A689 Slaggyford road angles north from the main A686 Penrith road. It begins as a driveway or track, then becomes a narrow path with the river and town to the right (east) and a field rising to moorland on the left. This path continues along the edge of a pasture through the old gates of Harbut Lodge **C**.

Old barn and byre above the South Tyne Valley near Wanwood, north-west of Alston.

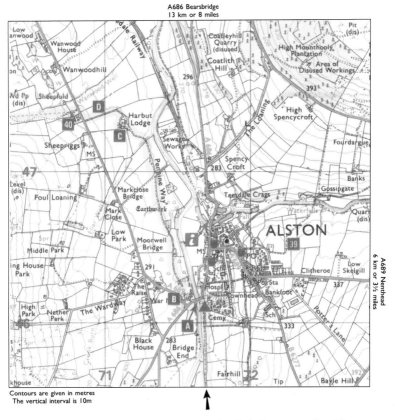

Contours are given in metres
The vertical interval is 10m

There is a detour at the lodge, to the left between buildings rather than past the front of the main house; this takes you around a small field past the coach house and over a step-stile on to a track **D**. The track leads up to the A689 and the Way then turns right (north) along this, before veering left (west) across a marshy field and through a gate to the right of an old barn **40**. The byre and barn have very old narrow glass windows and a stone-slabbed roof – features no longer appropriate to modern farming. White paint around the byre door was there so that cattle, and bleary-eyed milkmaids, could find their way in at pre-dawn milking time.

Just after the gate there is a little stream or sike, colonised by brooklime, a kind of speedwell with little blue flowers. The fleshy foliage is edible but uninviting – particularly in sheep country where liver-fluke, which spends part of its life cycle in water-snails, is endemic. Beyond the stream the Way heads uphill over pasture, leading to an elaborate ladder stile over a wall **E**. The official route now does a curious loop south-west

77

along the side of a drove road, then north-west down to the Gilderdale Burn, then north-east to pick up a footbridge. A farmer once ran a bull in the field and the Way had to be re-routed, but this is ancient history and it is a simple matter now to make for another of the monster stiles across the marshy pasture to the north-west **F**, then drop straight down to the footbridge **G** and so enter Northumberland. From here the Way climbs by a very muddy path, crossing a stile and heading uphill **H** to meet a track and bear left (north-west) through improved pasture and out on to the open fellside.

The Pennine Way arcs around the grassy ramparts of Whitley Castle **41**, a Roman fort built to defend a road linking the Stanegate at Carvoran with Watling Street at Kirkby Thore. Known as the Maiden Way, this road was probably laid about AD 80, after Agricola had blazed a trail northwards to crush the barbarians (see page 95). It is fascinating to see how dry stone walls cut straight across the fort as if it were not there; for centuries farmers, and the rest of society, had a total disdain for history and apparently worthless relics.

At Castle Nook **I** the path across a burn and down to the road has been obliterated and it may be necessary to walk through the farmyard. The road is, of course, the A689; the Way flirts or plays hide and seek with it all the way to Lambley, until it turns west at Halton Lea Gate.

Across the road and through a gate there is a path on the right side of a wall which leads to Dyke House **J**, at which the route clips the corner of an enclosure around a group of houses. It then regains the same line north-north-west along the top of the fields, with a wall to the left and the old South Tyne railway line to the right. At a gate where the wall ends **K** the route is obscure but goes straight on, across rough grassland to Kirkhaugh at which a tarmac track is followed left. After a group of buildings on the right, and well before the little Wesleyan chapel **42**, the Way turns right **L** and heads north-north-west in a straight line, across fields and stiles heading just to the left of the knoll of Lintley Farm **M**, then drops down to cross a footbridge over Thornhope Burn. The deep cleft of the burn has forced the trees to grow very tall; they compete at each other's expense to reach the light and make the streamside, and the five-arched viaduct **43**, a dark and damp place.

Nine viaducts were built to carry the Alston branch of the Newcastle–Carlisle railway. The line was built in the early 1850s, mainly to transport galena (lead ore) from the local mines

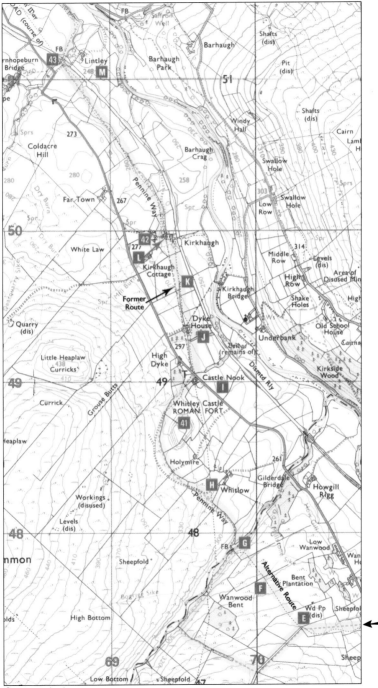

Contours are given in metres
The vertical interval is 10m

to Haltwhistle and thence to Tyneside. It was never a successful venture; by the 1880s lead production had slumped, though about 20,000 tons of coal from the Tindale Fell Colliery (west of Halton Lea Gate) kept the rolling stock occupied. For most of this century the line has been uneconomic and in 1976 it closed for good. It is now owned by the county council which manages it as a trail. The Way bears north-east around a field, following the bend of the Thornhope Burn, to meet the South Tyne again. The far bank of the river rises sharply through larch plantation and walled pastures which were enclosed in the land-grabbing of the 18th and 19th centuries. Above, the heather is topped by Wardley Law at an altitude of 1,552 feet (464 metres).

The South Tyne is restful rather than spectacular, and except in winter spate it rarely carries a great volume of water. It is usually wide, shallow and pebbly. A little way along the path you are introduced to this river in a delightful setting of riverside pasture, tumbledown walls and a bower of greenery. A pretty snapshot is marred by rubbish dumped along the far bank, creating an unfortunate impression of desecration; at the next bridge **N** the Way bears left to a road and forsakes the river which is never seen at close quarters again. The road is the A689, following the old track of the Maiden Way and leading into the village of Slaggyford **44** ('slaggy' means 'muddy').

Lambley Viaduct had a relatively short working life. It is now unsafe and is closed to any kind of traffic.

It is remarkable how many times authors on the Pennine Way nominate a Methodist chapel as a landmark or start point. Clearly, they were built at important places, and it is difficult to avoid them. From Slaggyford the Way leaves the third chapel of the day, leading down a track to its right **O**. This is a damp, deceptive track and botanical knowledge is useful; past hawthorn and ash trees all is well but a willow warns of wet ground – and so it proves as the track is hijacked by a little stream. Beyond this the Way dries out again through birch and hazel, then drops down to the Knar Burn and a blue footbridge, with a good view of another five-arched viaduct **45**. After this the Way crosses under the old railway line and then continues along a track to Merry Knowe **P** – through the gate and between buildings rather than to the right – then back into the farm grounds and over a step-stile in a wall.

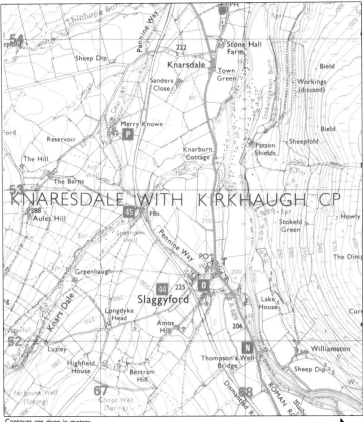

Contours are given in metres
The vertical interval is 10m

After following a wall for a short distance the Way crosses it at another stile and heads over pastureland, then crosses a road and makes its way over pasture again towards another viaduct **46**. Just before this a path bears right, down to a road, which is followed left across the Thinhope Burn until another track leads up past Burnstones and, via a spoil heap **Q**, arrives at last on open moorland. The panorama is excellent. Glendue Fell is to the left (west), part of an extensive block of moorland including the RSPB reserve of Geltsdale. To the north-east, across the wooded South Tyne Valley, Wallace's Crags stand out on Ashholme Common. To the south is the Cross Fell range.

Underfoot is the Maiden Way, well-defined. At last you really feel you are walking with Agricola's army. A wet foot soldier would have known that Carvoran and the comfort of the Tyne Valley were not so very far away but would probably have heard nasty stories about what lay beyond in the border wastes.

The Way keeps to the very edge of the moorland and soon drops down to renew its affair with the A689, then crosses an attractive stream, the Glendue Burn, before rising again to follow a fence along the moor edge of Lambley Common. This is a much wetter stretch, particularly on the plateau, where the heather is often sodden. Grouse abound – this is carefully managed moorland, regularly burnt – but there is also a high density of curlews and golden plovers and a good chance of seeing merlins or other birds of prey. Lambley, and its fine nine-arched viaduct **47**, lies in the valley to the north-east, but the north now beckons as the ridge of the Whin Sill, last seen in Teesdale, appears to the north-east, beyond the Tyne Gap.

The Way crosses the fence on the plateau, then keeps company with it until it recrosses on the descent **R** to the A689 west of Lambley village. Here it turns sharp west, then bears north down to the road, midway between the villages of Halton Lea Gate and Lambley. Once across the road the countryside is quite different. Moorland gives way to old mine workings.

CIRCULAR WALK: LAMBLEY AND THE SOUTH TYNE TRAIL

6 miles (9.5 km)

This is an easy walk. Park at Lambley village and walk down a wooded path to Lambley viaduct, then south along the course of the old South Tyne railway line to link with a moorland section of the Pennine Way.

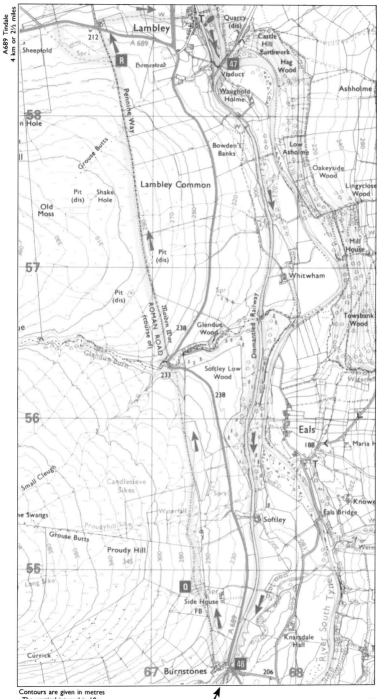

Contours are given in metres
The vertical interval is 10m

The Way is indistinct and boggy. Make for a grassy knoll, then for a post on the brow of the hill, then continue north-north-west to High House **S**, a ruined barn. From here descend along a grassy spur to cross the Hartley Burn at a blue bridge. For a little while the path keeps to the burn side, by alders and downy birches, before striking uphill to cut off the corner of the official Way, with Foxhole Cleugh to the west. The path is now across farmland, from stile to stile through pastures and the steading of Batey Shield, then down to a footbridge over the Kellah Burn and a side road and up a track to Greenriggs. The only problems are likely to be around the farm steadings, particularly at Greenriggs **T** where it is important to follow the route through the gate to the left (west) rather than the right (east) of the house.

This leads to another gate after which the Way climbs north-west up a field to a ladder-stile **U** before confronting a near-featureless block of moorland. This is Hartleyburn Common, leading to the even more daunting expanse of Blenkinsopp Common. A wet desert of hair-moss and coarse grasses drifts away in all directions; sheep have a hungry look, birds are few and silent. Take a bearing and walk north-west, heading a little to the left (west) of the brow of Round Hill **V**. From here keep the same bearing for 1½ miles (2 km) across rolling ground. The Pennine Way is distinct in most places but is unreliable. There are a few walls and fences, otherwise waves of wind-scorched grass stretch like dunes to the horizon. At the end of a long day

Batey Shield, north of Halton Lea Gate.

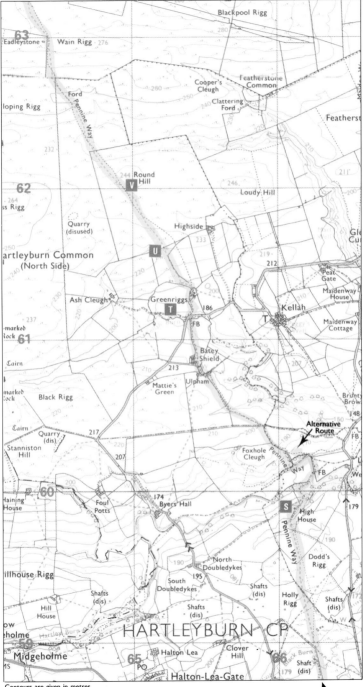

Contours are given in metres
The vertical interval is 10m

85

such a prospect may not lift the spirits, but a wilderness is always worthy of respect. Eventually a triangulation point appears on the skyline at Blade Hill **W**. Make for a point to the right of this after which the A69 Tyne–Carlisle road will be visible below.

This is a busy and dangerous road and the Way avoids the hazard by dropping down to Gap Shields **X**, then follows a muddy track through a gate, and detours south-east along a track under pylons, to ruined buildings and mine workings **Y**. It then heads downhill and back under pylons before meeting the road half a mile west of Greenhead village **48**. The quickest way into the village is to walk along the road (there is a new bypass, not marked on maps). However, for those continuing the walk, the Way crosses the road directly and leads up to a steep bank **Z**, then heads north-east and east across fields to meet the B6318, Gilsland road.

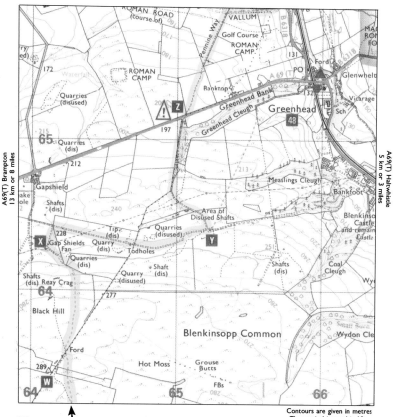

Contours are given in metres
The vertical interval is 10m

Birds of prey

Birds often help us to fix a memory of place in our minds; kittiwakes above a windswept cliff, turtle doves along a dusty southern lane. In the Pennines, the call of a golden plover or curlew can stir the spirit of a walker, but it is the sighting of a hawk or falcon that sends the heart racing.

Britain's birds of prey were decimated in the 18th and 19th centuries by gamekeepers. The only exception was the kestrel, a hovering mouse-killer never seen as a threat to pheasant or grouse and therefore ignored. In the 1950s an additional hazard, pesticides, wreaked havoc even among falcons nesting in remote and forgotten uplands, and changes in agriculture were beginning to reduce the suitable hunting territories. When the Pennine Way was established it might have been possible to walk the whole route without seeing a bird of prey at all. Now, it would take very bad luck or bad observation not to encounter one or two, even if only as nameless shadows over distant hills. However, even the briefest of sightings should provide a few clues to identification and a worthwhile memory to take away.

The commonest bird of prey in most uplands is the sparrowhawk, which nests in shelterbelts or forest plantations but ranges widely in search of food. The male is quite small and feeds on finch-sized birds; the female is much larger and takes anything up to pigeons and jackdaws. Sparrowhawks have broad blunt wings and a bullet-shaped body; they are usually seen flying very fast along hedges hoping to take prey by surprise, but sometimes they soar high over their territories, circling like miniature eagles.

In some places where there are extensive and mature conifer plantations, such as in north Derbyshire and south Northumberland, goshawks occur. These look like giant sparrowhawks and have similar hunting habits, but they are rare and elusive and have only recently become established after virtual extermination. A sighting on the Pennine Way would be fortunate indeed. Buzzards, by contrast, are among the easiest of birds of prey to locate; they are very big, enjoy soaring over open valleys and hillsides, and have a loud 'mewing' call. Again, trees are necessary for nesting, but in this case the requirement is for broadleaved woodland, and the bird is most common where there are relics or fragments of oakwoods on the sides of steep valleys, as there are above the Eden in Cumbria. In general, buzzards are increasing, but lack of habitat and continued keepering is preventing them from colonising most of Yorkshire and Northumberland.

Buzzards have a wingspan of up to 5 feet (1.5 metres). The only other long-winged bird of prey of comparable size likely to be seen over the Pennines is the hen harrier. At any time of the year wide expanses of open moorland may attract lone hen harriers. Their habit of quartering low over the ground, wings held in a shallow V, makes them easy to identify. The male is gull-grey with black wing-tips, the female and juvenile birds (much more likely to be seen here than adult males) are brown with a white rump. Pairs of harriers select young conifer plantations in which to nest, but they need large expanses of open hunting territory nearby and the Pennines are not particularly favoured. Persecution by gamekeepers is still one of the major problems.

Most walkers in the Pennines who see large birds of prey search among the pictures of hawks or buzzards in their field guides, but they would be better served looking among the owls, for it is the short-eared owl that is most likely to come to their attention. This is partly because it hunts methodically over a regular patch and is therefore easy to see, and partly because in most years it is tolerably common. The short-eared owl feeds on voles and its breeding success is dictated by the abundance of its prey, which means that it often has a bumper breeding surge followed by a disastrous crash. One year there are owls everywhere, the next year none.

Short-eared owls choose similar habitats to hen harriers both for nesting and hunting, which means the two species are often seen over the same block of moorland. However, the moth-like flight of the owl is quite unlike that of a hawk and its wings are broad and seem pale against evening heather. Unlike other owls the short-eared often hunts in broad daylight, especially if it is hungry or has a nestful of owlets to feed, but it is most often encountered in the early evening, silent as a ghost.

Finally, on the Pennines there are the falcons. These are sharp-winged and agile predators; even the kestrel, which nests as readily on crags as on trees, seems to enjoy the freedom of the open fells and has a dashing and purposeful flight. Most Pennine Way walkers hope to see merlins and peregrines but have to be content with kestrels. Fortunately, after many years of decline, a reduction in the use of toxic chemicals has resulted in a spectacular increase in the numbers of peregrines and many long-deserted crags have begun to echo to the 'kek-kek-kek' of nesting birds. Peregrines often stay close to their crags all year but they are free spirits and can turn up almost anywhere. The peregrine has a wingspan of over 3 feet (1 metre) and has a barrel-chest and broad wing-bases, yet its power is tempered by effortless grace and in flight it is easily the most impressive of Pennine birds. By contrast, the merlin is mercurial; it kills its prey by a chase rather than the hammer-blow of a stoop and its flight is low and very fast. It nests among heather or in low stunted pines but needs tracts of undisturbed moorland over which to hunt – hence it has become a rarity, even in the North Pennines. The male is grey and not much bigger than a large thrush, the female is brown and a little smaller than a kestrel.

Few places offer as good a chance of seeing birds of prey as the Pennines. Apart from the species that nest regularly along the route of the Way, there is always the chance of a migrant – a hobby, osprey, rough-legged buzzard or kite. The sky is a highway for such creatures and the Pennines are no barrier to them.

After coming close to extinction the goshawk has now colonised some of the mature spruce forests through which the Pennine Way passes.

Greenhead to Steel Rigg

6½ miles (10.6 km)

GREENHEAD   Carvoran   Cawfields Quarry

48————49————51————52————56————61——➤

     Thirlwall   Walltown   STEEL RIGG

     Castle   Quarry

If you are in a hurry this section can be walked in less than three hours, but life is too short not to use each day more wisely. Hadrian's Wall requires contemplation, and in any case the country through which it passes is more tiring than it looks. Give it a whole day and it will repay you in spectacular memories. On the other hand, if it is raining the exposed ridge upon which the Wall is perched is a misery. Pity the Romans, who knew it all too well. 'O me miserum' might have been etched into every stone.

Starting on the B6318, the Gilsland road north out of Greenhead **48**, the Way begins as a track beside a terrace of red brick houses, then crosses a railway line and the Pow Charney Burn **A**. It then arcs northwards to follow the larger Tipalt Burn round a field to Thirlwall Castle **49** and Duffenfoot. Without realising it you are already well into the stuff of history and legend, for the Wall once ran west–east across this field and the Pennine Way crosses its buried foundations just south of the castle. The flat ground marks a gap in the natural barrier of the ridge and was therefore a weak point in the Roman defences. It is here that Caledonian tribesmen are thought to have broken through, possibly during the Barbarian Conspiracy of 367.

Thirlwall Castle, a fortified tower-house dating back nearly 700 years, was built from stone dismantled from the Wall and the nearby Roman fort of Carvoran. Few people could afford to care about their historical heritage in the benighted Middle Ages. Edward I stayed here on 20th September 1306, during his wars against the Scots, and its menacing walls must then have seemed an oasis in a desert of squalid border poverty. But its era was brief. It has been ruinous for at least 300 years and part of it has already fallen into the Tipalt Burn.

The Pennine Way turns right in front of the castle mound, down to a footbridge where it crosses the Tipalt, then goes through a gate and passes Holmhead **B**, then climbs uphill through woodland along a walled track. At the end of this there is open pasture and the Way follows a wide, grassy ditch beside a wall. The ditch **50** was part of the Roman fortifications and ran along the northern side of the Wall. Another broad ditch called the Vallum marked the extent of the military zone to the south.

At the brow of the hill the Way crosses a ladder-stile and enters Northumberland National Park, continuing eastwards with a wall to the right. Beyond this is the unexcavated Agricolan fort of Carvoran **51**, beside the museum of the Roman Army. Dominating the view eastwards is the great quarry of Walltown **52** – once an ugly scar but healing nicely under the management of the Northumberland National Park. On the far brow, Hadrian's Wall can be seen for the first time **53**. If the grey cliffs look familiar it is because they are part of the Whin Sill, last encountered along the Pennine Way in Teesdale, and, as in Teesdale, several quarries worked the dolerite for roadstone. This serpent-backed ridge is known as the Nine Nicks of Thirlwall, but quarries have altered the silhouette and made the name less appropriate.

The Way meets a road and turns right along it, then turns left at a quarry hut **C** and crosses the corner of the reclaimed quarry site to meet a narrow, tarmacked side road. After following this until it passes a cattle grid **D**, the Way at last leads uphill to the crest of the ridge and a section of Hadrian's Wall.

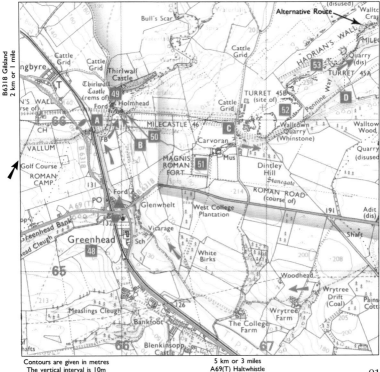

Contours are given in metres
The vertical interval is 10m

5 km or 3 miles
A69(T) Haltwhistle

A vivid imagination is essential to see the Wall in its original glory, for nowhere is it even half complete. However, the setting helps to create a suitable atmosphere, and this should be an exciting moment. Walking eastwards, the Way takes you along the crest of the Sill with the steep scarp slope, colonised by rowan, birch and aspen, to your left and the gentle dip slope to the right. The soil is quite thin and in places plates of whinstone are exposed. The deep fissures in these grey pavements are often green with moss and there are patches of wild chives – a rare plant supposed to have been introduced by the Romans.

The Wall itself flatters to deceive, for after a fine turret (44B) **54**, standing up to ten courses high, it dwindles to a few fragments or the ghost of a mound often topped by an ordinary dry stone wall. The official Way actually follows the line of the Military Way, a supply road, but it is worth staying faithful to the Wall path if only for the views north, across wastes and mires to Wark Forest.

Aesica (Great Chesters) Roman fort **55** comes as a surprise – most people find themselves walking through the middle of it

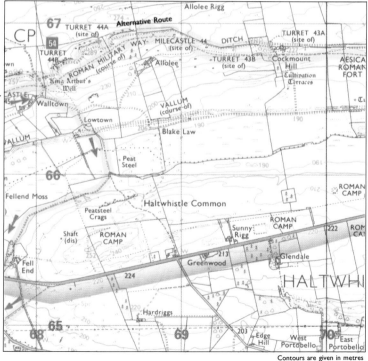

Contours are given in metres
The vertical interval is 10m

before they notice anything unusual. This and the total lack of information signs make it a refreshing place. Most of the Wall forts, including Aesica, post-date the first phase of building (the original idea here had been for a smaller milecastle) but they were written into the plans when it was found that the older forts of Vindolanda and Carvoran were too far away to allow for the necessary rapid deployment of troops.

From Great Chesters, the Way drops down, past a stone cottage **E** and over a ladder-stile on to the road, across the Caw Burn, then along a road **F** and past Cawfields quarry – now an attractive picnic site with toilets and a national park information caravan **56**. Once past the large pond, and a fine cross-section of the Whin Sill **57**, a path climbs back to the ridge crest and passes the stone skeleton of Milecastle 42 **58**, with an excellent stretch of the Vallum visible at the foot of the dip slope to the right **59**.

The subsequent walk along Cawfield Crags takes you along one of the best preserved sections of Hadrian's Wall, much of it having been renovated in the last century. After Caw Gap **G** it is

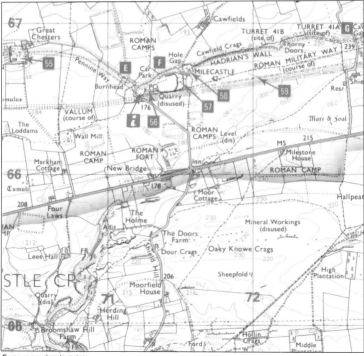

Contours are given in metres
The vertical interval is 10m

possible to get into a good stride along Windshields Crag to reach the highest point on the Whin Sill **60**. On a clear day you can see south across the Pennines, west over the Solway Firth, and north to the Cheviots. Unfortunately, clear days are depressingly few. The word 'shield' or 'shiel', in many local place names, is a leftover from the days when farmers used to spend the summer with their flocks, staying in huts out on the hills. This process, called transhumance, lasted until the 17th century and bred a poverty from which the area has hardly recovered.

From the triangulation point at 1,132 feet (345 metres) the Way quickly descends eastward to meet a side road **H**, after which it is possible to walk along the top of the Wall to the south of Steel Rigg car park **61**. If you intend overnighting at or near the Once Brewed Youth Hostel you can follow the Military Way to meet the side road a little further down the hill **I**, and turn down this to the main road, known as the Military Road or

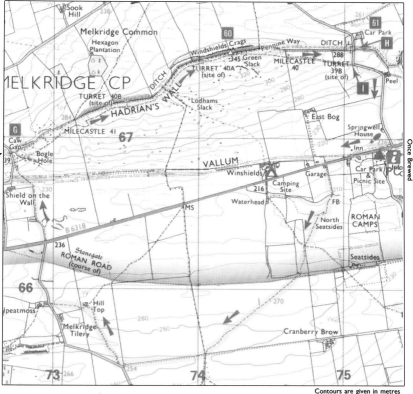

Contours are given in metres
The vertical interval is 10m

Wade's Road because it was built by General Wade to carry troops in the post-Jacobite years.

The youth hostel has a national park information centre to the east, and the Twice Brewed Inn to the west.

CIRCULAR WALK: HADRIAN'S WALL AND WALLTOWN

5¼ miles (8.5 km) (see maps on pages 91–2)
Park either at Walltown car park (north-east of the main quarry site) or along the B6318. From here the route passes Thirlwall Castle and follows the Pennine Way through Walltown quarry and along Hadrian's Wall, turning south and west through wet moorland and pastures to return via Greenhead.

CIRCULAR WALK: HADRIAN'S WALL AND ONCE BREWED

5 miles (8 km) (see map on page 94)
Park at the Once Brewed Information Centre and walk along the waymarked route through fields to the south of the B6318 (the Military Road). After crossing the line of the Stanegate Roman road, the walk crosses the B6318 and makes for Hadrian's Wall, from where it turns east along the Pennine Way along the high section of the Whin Sill.

The Romans

What would British history have been like without the Romans? Did the invasion of Claudius in AD 43 mark the end of an idyllic pastoral economy or the beginning of true civilisation? Perhaps both. Relics of the occupation once littered the country, but over the centuries the scars have healed. Only in the far north, especially across the rolling hills between the Tyne and the Tweed, are there clear signs of their endeavours. The Pennine Way acts as a transect to the remains and offers a unique insight into what it might have felt like to walk for days and arrive in a wilderness.

Agricola's army reached the North Pennines and Cheviot Hills in AD 80–1. By establishing a network of roads defended by forts and supply bases the legions were able to push further north into Caledonian territory and leave isolated pockets of resistance to be mopped up later. Many impressive Iron Age forts, visible today as rings of tumbled stones circling the tops of rounded Cheviot foothills, were bypassed in this way and were

Hadrian's Wall follows the crest of the Whin Sill, reaching its highest point here

at Whinshields Crags. In the distance is Crag Lough.

Steel Rigg to Bellingham

14¾ miles (23.7 km)

STEEL RIGG   Lowstead
61————64————75————80———→
Crag Lough   BELLINGHAM

The most dramatic start to any section of the Pennine Way begins from the national park car park at Steel Rigg **61**. Within a few minutes you are walking the Wall, taking a well-trodden path along the top of the broad, consolidated remains of Britain's most important ancient monument. You are not quite walking in the footprints of the Romans, for the Wall was much higher in their day, but you certainly have a clear sense of history beneath your feet. The switchback crest of the Whin Sill lies ahead, its steep north-facing scarp looking out over frost-shattered scree and the rolling 'cuesta' landscape towards the forests of Henshaw Common. Away to the south, across the Tyne Gap, are the Pennine moors of Whitfield and Cold Fell. This is a fascinating and threatening place. It must have seemed like the end of the world to the Romans, and it can be cold and windswept even in high summer.

The Way stays on the Wall top for only a few yards, after which it keeps close company beside it. The gap in the line of the Whin Sill before Peel Crags affords a good view of the grey face of quartz-dolerite, squeezed out as magma between beds of limestone and sandstone nearly 300 million years ago, then cooled and weathered into near-hexagonal columns. Below the rock face is a rubble of scree **62** colonised by such plants as parsley fern and club moss.

Peel Crags sets you into a good walking stride before dipping down into Castle Nick and Sycamore Gap, sharp clefts in the Sill created by Ice Age meltwater. The National Trust has been doing a great deal of restoration work in this area, involving temporary diversions to the Pennine Way, and both the Wall and Milecastle 39 **63** are in good shape. The loose stonework and whinstone boulders provide nesting sites for wheatears with their distinctive black-tipped tail and white rump. The name 'wheatear', which might seem inappropriate considering the habitat, began as a down-to-earth description, 'white-arse', but was cleaned up in Victorian times. The path over Highshield Crags, above Crag Lough **64**, runs on the north side of a wall (not The Wall, which is missing here), and close to the edge of the Whin Sill. Vertical chasms in the rock face add a hint of danger and should be negotiated with care.

The view of the lough is excellent. There are usually swans on the water, either whooper or mute depending on the time of year. Other wildfowl look very tiny from this height. The path, dry and firm underfoot, drops down through a plantation of pine, wych elm and sycamore, then leads out on to a track with the marshy eastern edge of the lough, colonised by willow, alder and birch, just to the left (north). Turn right, following the track through a gate **A**, then immediately leave the track and cross a ladder-stile to the left. There is now a rather steep pull, past the grass-covered remains of Milecastle 38 and Hotbank Farm **B**, up to Hotbank Crags. The Wall is again in good order, and it is possible to walk on it for a little of the way. Four lakes are visible from here. Away to the south-east is Grindon Lough, one of the best bird-watching places in the area (lots of wild geese, occasional hen harriers, peregrines and merlins), while north of the Wall there is Crag Lough (to the west), Greenlee

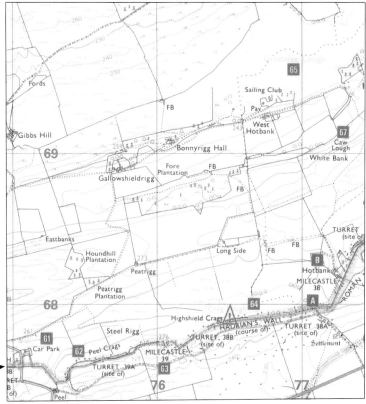

Contours are given in metres
The vertical interval is 10m

Lough **65** (to the north) and Broomlee Lough **66** (to the north-east). All these lakes are shallow and occupy basins created in the Ice Age when ice sheets creaked eastwards scouring out depressions in the bedrock. The fate of these attractive lakes is to become bogs; some old maps show Caw Lough **67**, this side of Greenlee, as open water, but nothing is now visible. In Roman times the wilderness north of the Wall must have been a land of lakes.

At Rapishaw Gap **C** the Pennine Way leaves Hadrian's Wall, thus depriving you of the most famous Wall view, towards Cuddy's Crags, and the finest excavated fort at Housesteads (Vercovicium) **68**. Is a detour recommended? On balance, no. It is a long way to Bellingham and there is always another day for sightseeing.

Released from the Wall, the Way heads north-north-east over marshy ground. The view back is a little disappointing, the crags not so dramatic and Housesteads barely visible on the dip slope. To the east the Sill rises to Sewingshields Crags (where King Arthur and his knights are supposed to be sleeping), then drops away like a spent wave on the shore of Tynedale. Ridley Common provides an unexpected interlude of heather and a pretty burn **69**, then the Way drops at Cragend to another burn

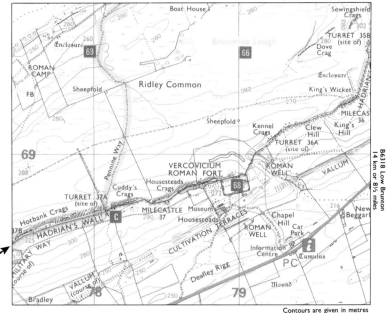

Contours are given in metres
The vertical interval is 10m

Rapishaw Gap is the natural cleft in the Whin Sill between Hotbank Crags and Cuddy's Crags.

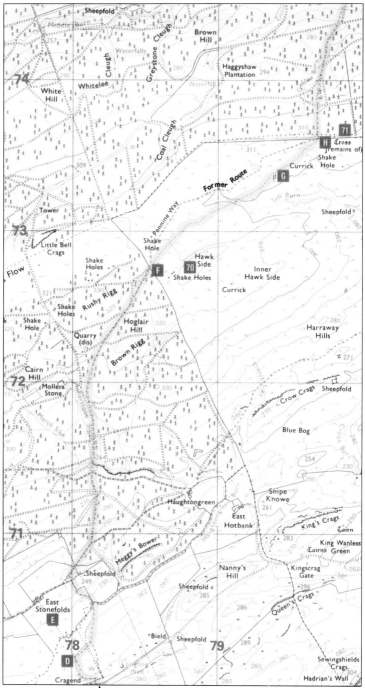

Contours are given in metres
The vertical interval is 10m

104

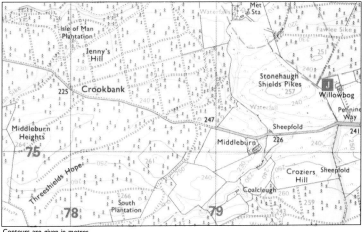

Contours are given in metres
The vertical interval is 10m

with a footbridge **D**. After this the path arcs eastward but it is indistinct and easily lost. Make for the forest to the north, with Greenlee Lough now visible to the west. Pass to the east of East Stonefolds **E**, then enter Wark Forest along a wide drive. The Way gains height steadily through the forest, along the drive then right along a path which leads out eventually at a step-stile and gate **F**.

This block of moorland, edged on three sides by spruce forest, has an eerie stillness about it, even on windy days. To the west is Bellcrag Flow, to the south is the heather-clad brow of Hawk Side **70**. Harriers, long-winged predators of open country, probably gave the place its name. Across the sea of wet moorgrass, make for the small group of stunted pines **G**. These lie within a winged sheepfold, so shaped to afford shelter from any gale. This makes an acceptable stopping point for lunch, though the desolation of the place may cause you to hasten on your way. A little to the east of where the Way re-enters the forest **H** there is a standing stone called Comyn's Cross **71**. Legend has it that the sons of King Arthur heard that their father had given a gold cup to a local chieftain, Comyn (or 'Cumming'), on his visit to Sewingshields. They rode forth to retrieve the gift, and slew the chieftain at this point.

From the stile leading back into the forest the prospect of Sitka and Norway spruce does not appeal, but a few steps further on there is a fine vista of more varied woodland, improved by the informal presence of larch. The Way leads down, crossing four tracks or drives and heading at first towards Ladyhill Farm **I**, then bearing to the west in line with Willowbog Farm **J** to lead out on a side road between Stonehaugh and the B6320.

After a short road walk the Way turns northward again along a forest track **K**, through spruce plantations, crossing two tarmac drives, before leading out again to open grassy moorland. The Pennine Way forms the boundary of Northumberland National Park between Ladyhill Farm and Bellingham, but route-finding may be difficult as wall-lines on the map do not correspond with what you see on the ground. There is little else to go on. Bear to the left of the brow of Ground Rigg **L**, then left down between hillocks, keeping to the upper right bank above Fawlee Sike (a 'sike' is a small stream).

If you have judged the route accurately you will find yourself beside a beautiful little waterfall **72**, a vertical cascade of up to 20 feet (6 metres), overhung with rowan, ivy and heather, with a misty basin of moss-covered rocks and shelves of hart's tongue and hard fern. A delightful spot and quite unexpected.

From here, follow the line of an old dyke or sod-cast ridge – the ghost of an enclosure hedge – crossing wet drainage channels by detouring to the left until eventually the Way leads over a ladder-stile across a wall, then downhill with grassy dykes to either side and towards the Warks Burn. A sharp right turn **M** through a gate and past a haybarn will bring you within sight of a footbridge **N**. The rock-lined Warks Burn lies in a deep, shady cleft. It is a pretty, birch-lined stream making its way eastwards to join the North Tyne below Wark village. The height of the cliff may not seem very terrifying but a few hundred yards upstream at Low Roses Bower there is a loo (or 'netty') corbelled over a 43-foot (13-metre) vertical drop, reputed to be the greatest in Britain. This uncomfortable prospect must have strengthened a few constitutions in its time, but the house has been derelict for years.

Once on the far bank of the burn, green pastures begin to dominate, and one small farm leads to another. Route-finding is straightforward but needs care around farm buildings where there might be signposted alternatives. Horneystead **73** dates back to 1837 and lies adjacent to the ruin of a fortified bastlehouse built about 1600 (see page 144). The Ash **74** is 18th to 19th century, with an elaborate Victorian conservatory or porch. Leadgate, on the side road to Wark, is of similar vintage. By far the most intriguing of the farms in the area is Lowstead **75**, perched over the east bank of the Blacka Burn. Around the little yard are grouped byres, stables and a cart shed and granary. The

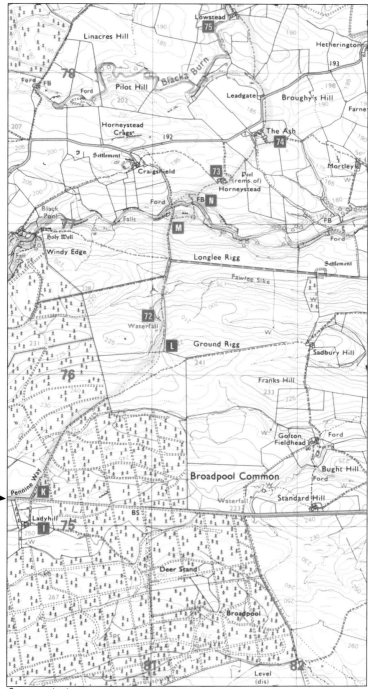

Contours are given in metres
The vertical interval is 10m

Lowstead has evolved from bastlehouses built in the days of Border conflict to

house, with its diamond-paned windows, and the adjoining byre to the left, are bastlehouses dating back to the 16th century. The 4-foot (1.2-metre) thick walls would have allowed the farmer and his family to sleep secure from 'reiving, riding Scots'.

A little way down the track above the Blacka Burn is Linacres, a modern, large, functional farm screened by tall trees. The Way follows the track eastwards **O**, then meets a road and follows this north-north-east, past a small quarry and limekiln on the left **76**. The hilly, close-cropped pasture on either side of the road is spectacularly 'cord-rigged', a mosaic of field systems dating back to Roman times. The uneven ground in the field corner marked on the map as a 'homestead' **77** (see page 109) was excavated in 1960 and revealed a typical Romano-British settlement comprising a rectangular enclosure and several circular stone huts. The fields all around were under cultivation to provide barley for the occupying garrison of the Wall forts. The land was farmed for at least 300 years, from the Iron Age to the fall of Rome, after which came the Dark Ages and a shadowy reshaping of society.

Where the road meets a T-junction **P** the Way continues north-east as a field path, alongside a fence and the remnants of

protect the inhabitants from rustlers and thieves.

a thorn hedge. After crossing the lines of three old sod-cast field boundaries the path heads downhill to cross the Houxty Burn at a footbridge **Q**, just downstream of Esp Mill. Once on the far

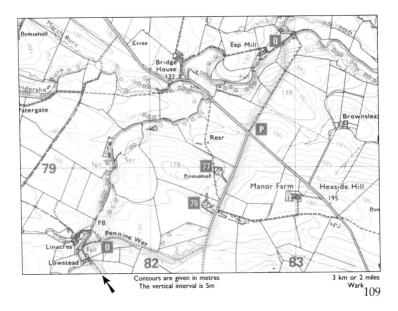

Contours are given in metres
The vertical interval is 5m

3 km or 2 miles
Wark

109

bank and past Shitlington Hall **R** (names can be misleading – it's only a farmhouse) the Way heads along a track, then uphill beside open pasture, then climbs the sandstone edge of Shitlington Crag and finally reaches a ladder-stile **S** in the wall to the left (west) of the tall radio mast. Beyond is a fine expanse of heather moorland on the crest of Ealingham Rigg, while to the south and south-west is a wonderful view of the route you have taken across the forgotten fields and forests north of the Wall.

After crossing the stile and walking along a track eastwards the Way suddenly heads out north-east across the rushy moorland **T** to make for a marker post on the brow of the hill, then, after crossing level ground, drops down again into the North Tyne Valley. The views of Bellingham, and the next section of the route, would round the day off nicely but there is an uncomfortable road walk remaining. The River North Tyne may deflect some of your irritation. It is a handsome river and is at its best between Bellingham and Wark. The old ford at Bridgeford **78** used to be the only all-year crossing, but the 'new' bridge **79** (built in the 1830s to replace one washed away in the Middle Ages) provides a suitable viewpoint. Ripples in the twilight may be caused by salmon or sea trout, by goosanders diving for eels, or by otters playing in the shallows. Up the hill and round the bend, Bellingham **80** with its inns and accommodation provides a very different tranquillity.

Rivers and burns

What happens to all the rain that falls on the Northumberland hills? Some of it certainly ends up in the boots of walkers but most of it is absorbed into a layer of peat and bog-moss. The water gradually seeps downhill through the blanket bog and gathers into narrow channels or 'sikes', which then run into streams or burns.

Most of the rivers with headwaters along the Northumberland stretch of the Pennine Way, such as the Coquet and the Aln, flow eastward to meet the North Sea, but after the last Ice Age the course of the North Tyne was deflected southwards, to capture the Rede and the Warks Burn which had probably fed into the Wansbeck. The North Tyne now meets the South Tyne near Hexham, then flows east to Newcastle and Tynemouth.

There are few natural lakes within sight of the Pennine Way, and these are small and diminishing each year as they are choked by bog-moss and carr or willow/alder scrub; the lakes or

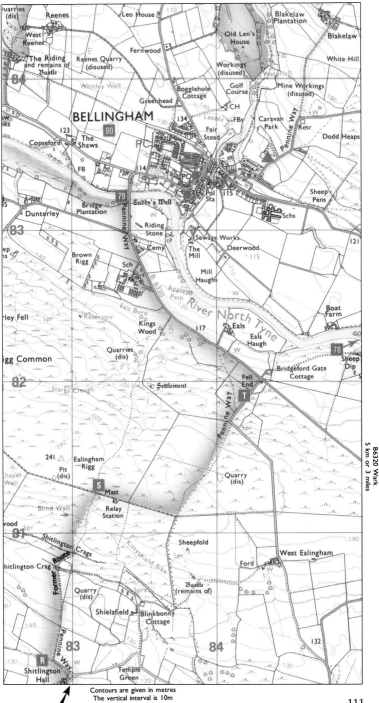

Contours are given in metres
The vertical interval is 10m

B6320 Wark
5 km or 3 miles

111

Warks Burn rises in the uplands of Northumberland National Park and meets the North Tyne below Wark village.

loughs (pronounced 'loffs') of the Hadrian's Wall area lie in the basins hollowed out by moving ice and they are shallow and reed-lined. Their visual impact in such a stark and stony landscape is considerable.

The gradient from the hilltops to the coast is quite steep, so once rainwater has filtered its way through marshy grassland and blanket bog into sikes and runnels it tumbles quickly down well defined rocky burns and sometimes cuts deep rocky gorges, as in the Warks Burn and the Hauxty Burn south of Bellingham. Water derived from rain soaking through the spongy layer of peat is acidic and the bedrock is mostly sandstone or andesite. This means the upland burns are poor in dissolved nutrients, though they are cold and turbulent and therefore rich in oxygen. These factors, together with the problem of coping with winter spates and summer droughts, mean that wildlife has to be well adapted. One of the most characteristic plants of stony riversides is the monkey flower, which originates from California, while the upper, shady banks of rivers often have patches of the beautiful melancholy thistle and giant bellflower. In some places, especially on the South Tyne where there has been contamination by heavy metals from lead mining activities, riverside grassland contains extensive patches of the mountain pansy.

Among the mammals, the water vole is uncommon but the otter, which has disappeared from most of England due to the effects of toxic chemicals and habitat destruction, is still widespread here. The North Tyne is one of the best rivers in the country for otters, as it is for salmon and sea trout.

The number of waterside birds decreases with altitude. Along the lower reaches of the larger burns there are sand martins, common sandpipers, oystercatchers and herons, and also goosanders, which were first recorded as British breeding birds on the River Coquet in the 1950s and are now found throughout Northumberland. Nesting birds of the rocky and turbulent upper reaches are limited to dippers and grey wagtails, and a few intrepid mallards.

The rich riverside flora of the North Tyne includes the impressive melancholy thistle.

From Shitlington Crag the landscape north of the Wall resolves itself into rolling

pastures and forest.

Bellingham to Byrness

BELLINGHAM   Whitley Pike   BYRNESS
80————82————90————95————97——→
Hareshaw   Blakehopeburnhaugh
Dene

14¾ miles (23.7 km)

Bellingham **80** (pronounced 'Bellinjum') is a grey little town of 1,000 souls. Among the shops and inns there is a 13th century Church of St Cuthbert, with an unusual stone-slabbed roof, constructed centuries ago to replace previous ones burned down in Scottish raids (see page 143). There is also a memorial in the market square **81** to local heroes who fell in the Boer War and, nearby, a curious mounted gun called a gingall, brought back from the Boxer rebellion in China.

From the centre of Bellingham the Pennine Way follows the West Woodburn road, downhill and across a bridge **A** over Hareshaw Burn. There is a reminder, in the shape of a signpost, that the route continues along the road. A track alongside the burn and through a national park car park leads to Hareshaw Dene **82**, a beautiful valley clothed in ancient wych elms and oaks. The route once took this course to allow a visit to Hareshaw Linn, one of the most attractive waterfalls in the country. Common sense dictates the diversion, relegating the Dene to an optional extra, perfect for an evening stroll but impossible to enjoy as an early detour before a long day.

Just after the bridge over Hareshaw Burn is the old course of the Border Counties Railway line **83**, constructed in the 1850s and 1860s to carry coal and iron ore. It was never profitable; once the industries had gone the line relied upon passengers and farm stock. The axe finally fell in 1956.

Uphill out of the town, the Way at last leaves tarmac **B**, heading north when the road goes east. The rounded mounds east of the junction are spoil heaps **84**, weathered green by the years, grass having formed a callus over the scarred landscape. Iron from the Hareshaw Iron Company furnaces was used in the construction of the High Level Bridge in Newcastle, but the enterprise was short-lived, opened in 1838 and closed just 10 years later.

Up the farm road, the wooded cleft of Hareshaw Dene is visible across the fields to the west. The Way eventually turns through the middle of Blakelaw farmyard **C**, past a lovely jumble of old and new buildings: stone troughs, pigsties, farrowing crates and gathering pens, asbestos and metal sheds and painted woodwork.

On the other side, with a lime kiln in the field away to the north-east, the Way gains height up an open grassy hillside, to an isolated post, then past the corner of a stone wall **D** and over the grass-decked spoil of old coal workings. On the skyline there is a pine plantation; to the right (east) of this is a stone ruin **E** and the gate that leads the Way back on to high moorland.

Boulders among the grass just beyond the gate have been colonised by some fine lichens, most notably *Peltigera*, a large, foliose ('leaf-shaped') species, but as the path leads downhill and back into Northumberland National Park the vegetation changes to rushes and moss.

Contours are given in metres   6 km or 3½ miles
The vertical interval is 10m   B6320 Wark

117

The Way forks here **F**, the official route making for the higher ground with Callerhues Crag to the east **85**, while an alternative route, well signposted at each end, keeps to the lower ground above Hareshaw Burn. The object of the new route is to avoid disturbing stock in the enclosure of Hareshaw House **86**.

North of the farmyard the Way continues along a wide track **87**, the ghost of a small coal-carrying railway line, past a quarry and workings and out on to the B6320 (west to Bellingham, east to the A68 and Otterburn). The Pennine Way crosses directly, north-north-east past an old mine and its spoil heap **88**. Coal was mined extensively in North Tynedale, but not on a sufficient scale to have any lasting impact on the countryside. The circular stone enclosure away to the west predates any industrial relics and is a kind of sheepfold, called a 'stell'.

The ground rises steadily, from mat-grass to heather, and there are few obvious landmarks except for grouse butts away to the east **G**. Make for the cairn on the distant brow of the hill.

Hareshaw Linn lies at the head of a beautiful tree-lined valley.

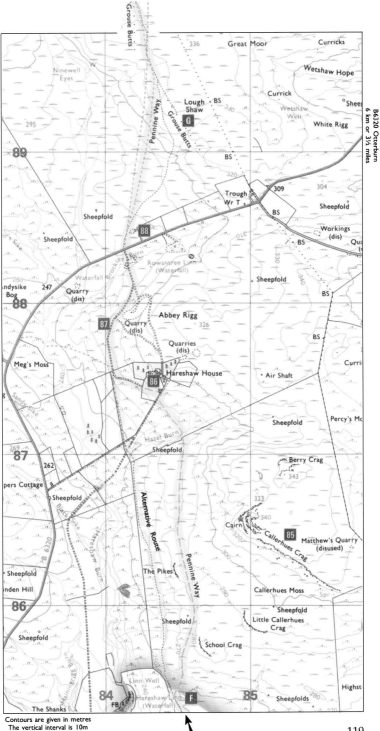

Contours are given in metres
The vertical interval is 10m

119

Rough pasture and open moorland west of Padon Hill.

The hill is Deer Play **89**, a wide wilderness with limitless views. A stone post **H** provides a good stopping place for lunch, after which the descent introduces another problem. The official route heads west-north-west then north along a fence-line to Whitley Pike. This route is seldom, if ever, used and it is a better idea to follow a north-west path, indistinct and boggy in places, which leads more directly to the cone of Whitley Pike **90**.

Once on the summit of this hill look for a direct path to the north-west, not along the official route by the fence-line but straight downhill over unavoidably marshy ground, making for a cattle grid and gates over an unfenced road **I**.

Route-finding is much easier now as the Way follows a fence for several miles. As the fence leads north-west on the straightforward ascent of Padon Hill there is a large sandstone boulder **91**, its surface heavily weathered. Bronze Age inhabitants of these hills often carved 'cup and ring' marks on to such stones, but so far nobody has claimed that any of the sculpted marks on the Grey Mare rock are anything other than natural. However, the summit of Padon Hill bears a very obvious man-made feature, a bell-shaped tumulus **92** built in the 1920s by the Morrison-Bell family who once owned nearby Otterburn Hall. Most of the stones used for the cairn would already have been on the hilltop; Padon Hill got its name from Alexander Peden, a Scottish Presbyterian who held services in out of the way places. This was in the reign of Charles II when Nonconformists, especially Scots, were repressed. Local people attending the illicit gatherings were requested to carry a stone with them up the hill to add to a growing symbol of defiance.

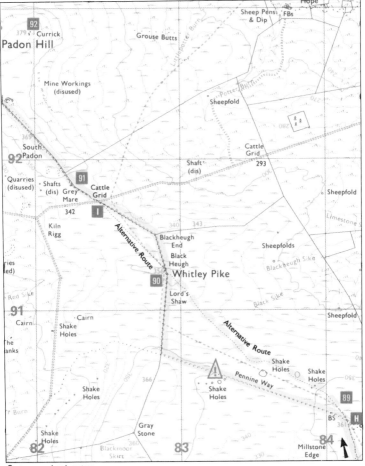

Contours are given in metres
The vertical interval is 10m

The large caterpillar of an emperor moth is surprisingly well camouflaged among summer heather.

The Way passes to the west of the brow of the hill, but a stile over the fence allows access to the 'pepperpot' cairn and provides excellent views over Redesdale. Due east is Otterburn, and just to the north of the village is the site of the Battle of Otterburn, fought in 1388 between the Scots and the English, at which the Earl Douglas of Scotland was killed and Sir Henry Percy ('Harry Hotspur', son of the Duke of Northumberland) was captured. The story of the battle – a Scottish victory – is told in a ballad popularised by Sir Walter Scott.

From Padon Hill the route keeps to the fence, with heather all around. The block of moorland always has a high population of emperor moths. This beautiful creature, the only British member of the silk moth family, is on the wing on sunny days in April and May. The massive caterpillar, green with black bands and covered with short bristles, is seen in late summer. It feeds on heather but enjoys sunning itself on the bare ground, where it either intrigues or terrifies walkers.

The Way drops down to a marshy saddle **J**, then rises via a steep little ascent to Brownrigg Head **93**. There are fine views north-east to the Cheviot massif, and south to Padon Hill, but ominous plantations of spruce trees begin to make an impact on the landscape; to the north-west stretch many miles of the Kielder complex of Forestry Commission land, while the steading of Gib Shiel to the west has become encircled by a private forest plantation. For some distance the Way continues with forest on one side and open moorland on the other. Occasional stones bearing the letters GH set the bounds on the old Redesdale estate of Gabriel Hall, High Sheriff of Northumberland in 1705.

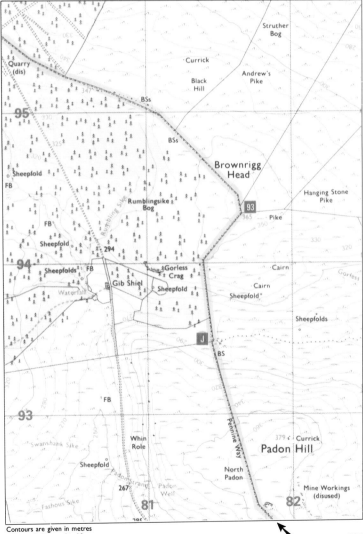

Contours are given in metres
The vertical interval is 10m

Eventually the route arcs westwards and becomes enclosed by trees. The twilight world of Kielder is entered at Rookengate **94**. Most walkers feel a sense of foreboding at this point. The notice somehow makes this worse; perhaps it should quote Dante – 'All hope abandon, ye who enter here'.

Once through the gate and on the wide forest drive, things do not seem quite so bad; the ground is firm and any wind and weather is elevated to the treetops. Vistas along rides reveal high hills to the north and moorland to the east, and there is a constant twitter of birds – mostly coal tits and chaffinches, but also crossbills. There is a chance of seeing sparrowhawks or even goshawks, predators which benefit from the seclusion of the forest.

The only constant features are the main drives and the little stone bridge over Greymare Sike **K**; the trees come and go, *en masse*. After several miles the drive descends, the green pastures of Redesdale at last appearing through the trees to the

A young conifer plantation above Gib Shiel.

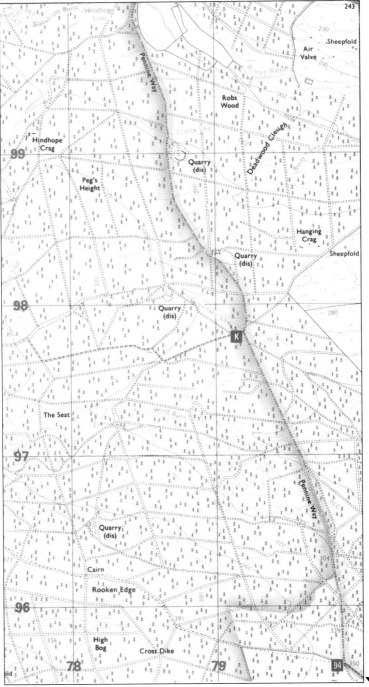

Air
Valve

Sheepfold

River Rede

Robs
Wood

Pennine Way

Hindhope
Crag

Clatty Sike

Deadwood Cleugh

99

Quarry
(dis)

Peg's
Height

Hanging
Crag

Sheepfold

Quarry
(dis)

98

Quarry
(dis)

K

The Seat

Wind Burn

97

Pennine Way

Quarry
(dis)

Quarry
(dis)

Cairn

Rooken Edge

96

High
Bog

Cross Dike

78

79

94

Contours are given in metres
The vertical interval is 10m

north-east. The farmstead is Blakehopeburnhaugh **95**, its buildings and land now owned by the Forestry Commission. The name has appeared in the *Guinness Book of Records* for many years as the longest place name in England. The elements are simply explained. 'Blake', black; 'hope', a fertile strip of valley land; 'burn', stream; 'haugh', low-lying land by a river. After miles of spruce plantations this is a pleasant and verdant place. The Blakehope Burn is peaty and handsome, and a little further on is a bridge **L** over the River Rede ('rede' means 'red', another reference to the colour of the water). According to most Pennine Way maps the route passes uphill after the bridge, but in practice this is impossible and merely leads on to the busy A68 and a tedious road walk to Byrness. Much better to keep to the east bank of the Rede, along a riverside with deciduous trees towards Cottonshopeburnfoot, then across a bridge **M** to the west bank and continue along a forest track through a plantation before turning downhill **N**, across the Rede again and past a picnic site and the beautiful little Holy Trinity Church **96**.

Incidentally, recent maps show Cottonshopeburnfoot as one word where it used to be two – hence it should displace Blakehopeburnhaugh as the longest place name.

Byrness village **97** is a curious little settlement of terraces built by the Forestry Commission in the 1930s. It may lack style but it is a welcome sight and has all the necessities for tired walkers.

The Border Forest

Conifers have an honourable place in the northern landscape; juniper and pine were once more widespread here than oak and there was a time, before the last Ice Age, when Norway spruce was a true citizen of the hills. These days it is fashionable to view conifer plantations with contempt, which is to damn by association some of the most beautiful landscape features in Scotland and the Lake District. Unfortunately, it would take a miracle for the peaty-gley soil of Kielder to yield anything but pulp-mill fodder and the impression from the Pennine Way is of an unwholesome world of spindly trunks and gloomy shadows.

Kielder Forest was a panic response to timber shortages after the First World War. Blocks of spruce trees were planted across the whole landscape irrespective of contours, water-courses or hilltops. The Forestry Commission was charged with a simple economic remit which did not embrace such novel concepts as conservation. Over the last few years attitudes have changed and the future is a little brighter; as the present even-aged forests reach maturity the age structure is being broken up and new plantations are being shaped around landscape features. Alder, birch and rowan trees are being planted along watercourses and footpaths (but not the Pennine Way, yet) and sites of special scientific interest are now managed sensitively or have been handed over to conservation agencies. But the essential business of the Forestry Commission will always be to produce timber. By the end of the century its 200 square miles (518 square km) of landholdings at Kielder will be producing 300,000 tons per year, most of it to be pulped for newsprint or shredded for chipboard. At present about 70 per cent of the forest is

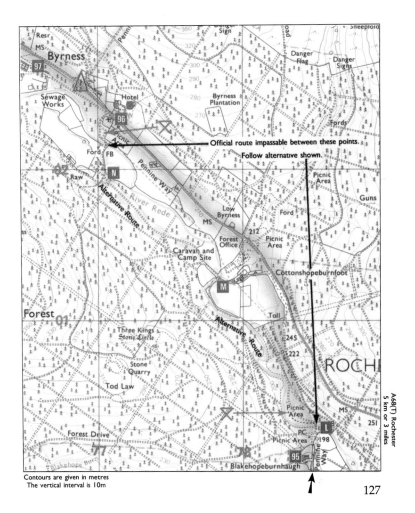

Contours are given in metres
The vertical interval is 10m

The Forestry Commission village of Byrness with Catcleugh Reservoir to the

composed of Sitka spruce, 15 per cent is Norway spruce, 9 per cent is lodgepole pine, and less than 1 per cent is native broadleaf species. In the future the composition will be 80 per cent Sitka, 2 per cent Norway spruce, no lodgepole, and about 10 per cent broadleaf trees, such as alder and sycamore.

When planting began in 1926 it was anticipated that forest industries would employ thousands of people, so special villages of terraced houses were built at such places as Stonehaugh and Byrness. Mechanisation, and the invention of the chain saw, has resulted in a massive reduction in the workforce and most of the houses have now been sold or stand empty. The Forestry Commission at Kielder employs a staff of only about 170 people, although there are many sub-contractors and associated industries which enhance the local economy.

One of the most damning criticisms of conifer plantations is that they are virtually lifeless. This is quite untrue in that there

north-west.

are always more birds and animals in an acre of forest than an acre of moorland. However, chaffinches and goldcrests do not have the same charisma as golden plovers and merlins, and the moorland habitat is diminishing at an alarming rate. Among the animals to benefit from the forest are red squirrels, roe deer and foxes, and there is a strong likelihood that wildcat and pine marten will soon be recolonising the border hills via the forests. Young conifer plantations are excellent for nesting birds such as short-eared owls and hen harriers but mature spruce forests are poor; crossbills, which are common locally, and goshawks, which are rare, are the icing on a very dull cake.

Finally, it is worth remembering that the Forestry Commission does not have a monopoly on growing trees. Most new plantations, in square regimental blocks, are the work of commercial forestry groups. It will be interesting to see how new government and EEC policies will affect land use in the uplands.

Byrness to Clennell Street

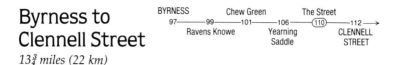

BYRNESS   Chew Green   The Street
97———99———101———106———(110)———112 —→
         Ravens Knowe   Yearning   CLENNELL
                          Saddle   STREET

13¾ miles (22 km)

The village of Byrness **97** was created for workers, first to build Catcleugh Reservoir, then to plant the Border Forest. As the trees of Kielder grew, the hamlet melted into the darkening forest. The number of foresters required to manage the plantations gradually decreased, so that several of the houses fell vacant or were sold. The youth hostel occupies a prime position in the stark terrace, while farm cottages and guest-houses provide alternative overnight accommodation. Byrness is a stop-over on most all-the-way itineraries because it precedes the Cheviot traverse. To complete the walk to Yetholm in a final day of 27 miles (43 km) is hard; an alternative, followed for convenience in this book, is to be picked up by prior arrangement at Rowhope or drop down for an overnight stay in Coquetdale. There are additional access points at Chew Green (west by public road through Coquetdale or east along a private MOD road, often open to the public during the spring and summer), or by dropping down to the north of the Border Ridge along Clennell Street into Cocklawfoot.

The A68 is a notoriously fast and dangerous road. The Pennine Way crosses it from the Holy Trinity Church **96** by heading north-west alongside it for 50 yards then up a tarmac path to a gate beside Byrness Cottage **A**. From Byrness village a short road walk south-east, crossing to a wide tarmac drive, leads up to the same gate. From the gate cross a field, then go through another gate and across a forest drive, then head uphill on a path through a mixed conifer plantation. The path is steep and straight, an excellent start because it takes an uncompromising line and wastes no time in gaining height and leaving the forest behind. After a short scramble up a rock edge the brow of Byrness Hill is reached. The lower courses of a stone fire look-out tower and the concrete base of a hexagonal hut **98** show how useful this place has been for a view over the Border Forest. By turning your face to the north you are suddenly at the threshold of a very different world, an open ridge often hammered by wind and rain and leading to the loneliest of hills in the least-populated part of England.

The Way heads north-west, along the broad crest of the ridge, from Saughy Crag to Houx Hill **B**. To the west is the head of

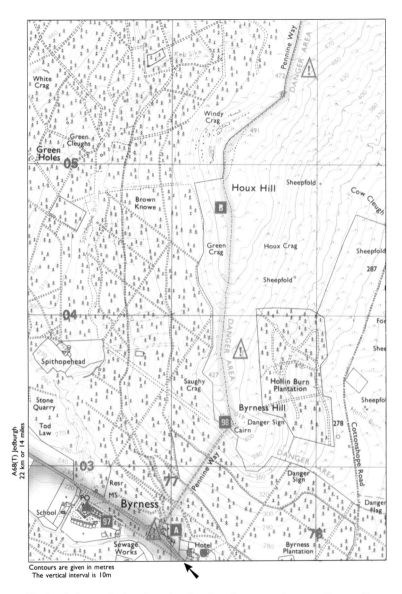

Redesdale, culminating in the Border crossing at Carter Bar. Catcleugh Reservoir sparkles like whetted steel against the deep green of the surrounding forest. Built at the turn of the century when 1,000 workers were employed for 15 years, it still supplies Tyneside with water; nearby Kielder Water may be 20 times the size but it was surplus to requirements even before it was completed in 1982.

The next high point along the Way is Ravens Knowe **99**. Ravens no longer nest here – keepers and shepherds carry a heavy burden of responsibility. The word 'knowe' means 'hill' – usually not a very big one. 'Law', as in Emmet Law to the east, means much the same thing. The view from Ravens Knowe is excellent, especially to the east, across the basin of the Cottonshope Burn to Loan Edge. This is Ministry of Defence property and signs warn of the dangers of trespass. The message on some of the signs is simple – 'Do not touch anything. It may explode and kill you.' The MOD owns 20 per cent of Northumberland National Park, a paradox that has brought criticism and controversy ever since the Park was created in 1956. The path itself is completely safe, and the whole block of land north of the Coquet is now a 'dry training' area with no live ammunition, but inevitably one's impression of the place is blighted.

The Way keeps to the high ground, to Ogre Hill with Harden Edge to the east. It then descends over boggy ground to the border fence, a well-worn path following the fence-line north-north-west with the official route to the east, and crosses a step-stile **C** into Scotland. Were it not for the forested slope of Ogre Hill this would be a featureless waste; the exact line of the border is arbitrary, depending on where each generation of farmers has replaced the fence.

Once, the Pennine Way turned north-east here to follow the sodden flow of the Coquet's headwaters **100**, but now the path leads north for a few hundred yards, then forks right **D** to drop down obliquely and meet a wicket-gate **E** above the more clearly formed Coquet. There is a great reluctance to lose height so dearly earned but the sacrifice is worth while as the route takes you around Chew Green **101**, a sprawling green maze of low earthworks marking Roman marching camps. The Pennine Way leads east, with the Coquet below and grass-covered ramparts above, then bears north-west around the edge of the earthworks. Coquetdale can now be seen as a steep-sided valley of interlocking spurs, one of the main arteries radiating from the heart of the Cheviot massif, to meet the North Sea at Amble.

It is unnecessary to follow the official Pennine Way route towards the Coquetdale road, unless you have arranged transport to make good your escape (this is the only place on this section of the Way close to vehicle access, though even here the uphill direction, along the line of the ancient Gamel's Path **102**,

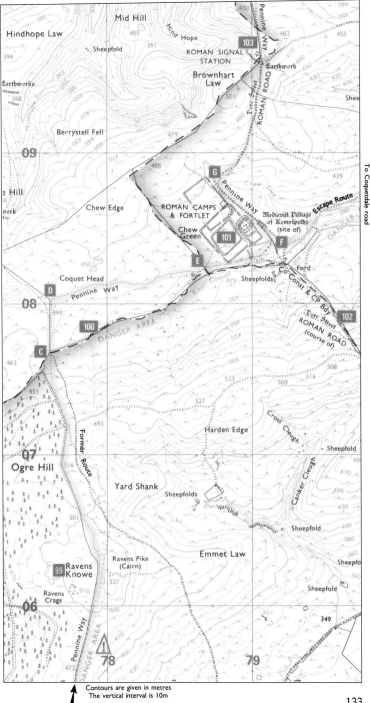

Contours are given in metres
The vertical interval is 10m

133

is a private MOD road to Redesdale and out of bounds if red flags are flying). Instead, turn left uphill **F**, alongside or among the ghosts of Roman billets and parade grounds. There is little left except the spirit of futility, of Shelley's 'Ozymandias' – 'Look on my works, ye Mighty and despair!' Chew Green was a stopover on a previous long-distance route, the perilous road from York to the Caledonian wilderness.

Halfway up the hill the Way bears north-east **G** to pick up the shadowy trackway that was Dere Street, and follows this to the Border fence to the north-east of Brownhart Law, close to a Roman signal station **103**. The Way stays with Agricola's road for a little longer, heading northwards along the Border Ridge. Rainwater falling on the Scottish side drains into Hindhope Burn, and thence into the Kale Water and the Teviot, which meets the Tweed at Kelso. Thus, west Scottish rain ends by flowing east to meet the North Sea at Berwick. Dere Street crosses the border at a five-bar gate **104** and makes its way down to the Kale by skirting Gaisty Law, Hunthall Hill and Woden Law. The Pennine Way stays on the high ridge and makes for a mound with a peat-built cairn and a post **H**. A clear path then leads north, obliquely away from the Border fence arcing eastwards via stone cairns and posts, and across marshy ground with short boardwalks over sikes and burns. The vegetation is sparse, composed of mat-grass and heather, apparently lifeless and unappealing, but for centuries herds of wild goats have survived in the Cheviots, as far from civilisation as they can get. After the October rut they range down into the valleys searching for better grazing. How long the goats have been here is a mystery – perhaps they were introduced by the monks of Lindisfarne. Certainly the domestication of goats dates back to the New Bronze Age, and feral or semi-wild herds have been roaming this lonely range of hills for at least 1,000 years. Wild goats come in many shapes and sizes, but are most often grey. The billies are big, long-horned, long-haired and seedy-looking.

The Way crosses some very boggy ground at the head of Rennies Burn **I** and there are some curious basins of *Molinia* grass **105** looking like mouldy pink porridge and known to walkers as the 'Grassy Loughs'. *Molinia* or purple moor grass is inedible or unappetising to most livestock, and much of the afforestation in Northumberland, particularly in the area to the north of the Wall, has taken place on impoverished 'prairieland' because it is good for nothing else. However, on this open ridge the scenic quality of the grass is far more significant.

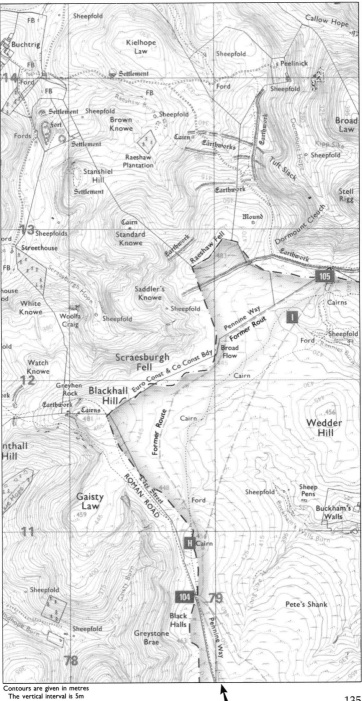

Contours are given in metres
The vertical interval is 5m

135

Back along the Border fence, now heading east, you start to notice the widening views, which are very fine. To the Scottish side are the fertile lowlands of the Teviot valley and Tweedsdale, the characteristic profile of the Eildon Hills by Melrose, and in the far distance the Lammermuir and Moorfoot Hills that bar the way to Edinburgh. On the English side the andesite foothills of the Cheviots obscure any view of the east coast.

At a fence corner the Way turns sharp left **J**, north-north-east, and drops down over tussocky grass to a gap in the Border Ridge called Yearning Saddle. A wooden shelter **106** is maintained here for the use of walkers, and it makes a welcome stopping place, out of the piercing wind.

The word 'Yearning', as in Yearning Law, the hill to the south-east, may be derived from the Anglo-Saxon word 'erne' meaning 'soarer', and applied especially to the white-tailed eagle. Golden eagles are occasionally seen over the border hills and moors, but the white-tailed eagle was lost to Britain over 60 years ago and its reintroduction still hangs in the balance. There are other bird names among these hills; Gowkhope ('gowk' is

The Border Ridge, from Lamb Hill to The Cheviot.

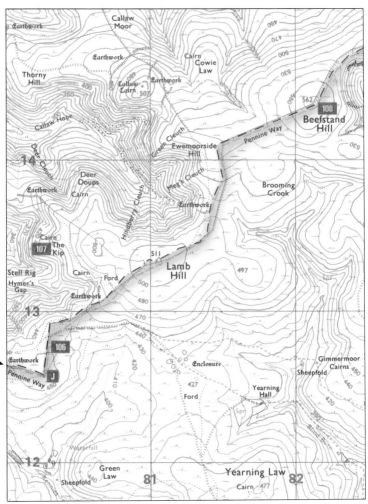

Contours are given in metres
The vertical interval is 10m

cuckoo), Cushat Law ('cushat' is woodpigeon), Cocklaw ('cock' is woodcock), and Corbies Crag ('corbie' is carrion crow) are clear examples.

From Yearning Saddle and its view of 'The Kip' **107**, above Kipp Sike to the north-west, the Way follows the Border fence faithfully for several miles, deviating only to cut obvious corners. The ridge links a chain of high hills including Lamb Hill, Beefstand and Mozie Law. From Beefstand **108** there is a classic view of the cold granite heart of the Cheviots, the wide whaleback of The Cheviot itself, flanked by Hedgehope and The

The climb from Coquetdale along The Street is one of the finest walks in the Cheviot Hills.

Schil. Mozie Law **109** is heathery with peat hags, the broad headwater allowing rainwater to seep south into the Coquet or north to Heatherhope Burn and its little reservoir. The route cuts off a fence corner before Plea Knowe **K**, then leaves the fence again to avoid a marshy patch called Foul Step (Pennine Way walkers were not the first to experience the blanket bog of the Cheviots; there are several other 'foul steps' in the area). Away to the south is a beautiful grassy ridge linking Black Braes to Swineside Law and Coquetdale. The clear track along the crest of the ridge is The Street **110**, an ancient drove road at its busiest before the Border troubles which started 700 years ago (see page 143). It is possible to follow this venerable green road down into Coquetdale to find accommodation at a farm or shepherd's cottage, but the total detour would be 6 miles (10 km) with a loss of at least 820 feet (250 metres) in height. Dire emergency would be the only reason for this course of action, though as part of a circular walk out of Coquetdale, from Windyhaugh, this path has distinct possibilities (see page 140).

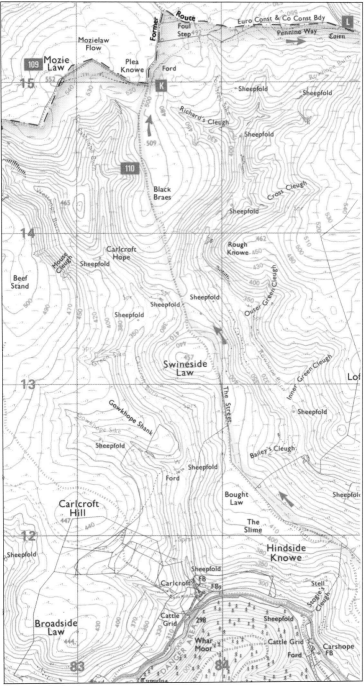

Contours are given in metres
The vertical interval is 10m

139

Ahead now is Windy Gyle, one of the most elegant and enigmatic of the Cheviot summits at a very respectable 2,030 feet (619 metres). It has a steep, sweeping slope southwards to the Rowhope Burn, beyond which the main features are the conifer plantation of Carshope and the cairned dome of Thirl Moor. The ascent of Windy Gyle is direct, straight up beside the fence line, then crossing at a stile **L** on to the Scottish side and continuing up to the cairn. The great Bronze Age mound of stones is called Russell's Cairn **111**, commemorating Lord Francis Russell, killed here during a wardens' meeting in 1585. Desolate and often snow-swept, and with violent and sinister associations, Windy Gyle is one of the atmospheric highlights of the Pennine Way. It is, quite literally, miles from anywhere.

CIRCULAR WALK: THE STREET, AN ANCIENT DROVE ROAD ACROSS THE BORDER RIDGE

8½ miles (13.5 km) (see maps on pages 139 and 141)
Park above the River Coquet close to Windyhaugh and walk up a green track to meet the Border Ridge. From here the route follows the Pennine Way to Windy Gyle then descends along an indistinct grassy path down into Coquetdale. The wonderful views make up for what can be quite a steep climb.

Dusk on the Border Ridge at Windy Gyle.

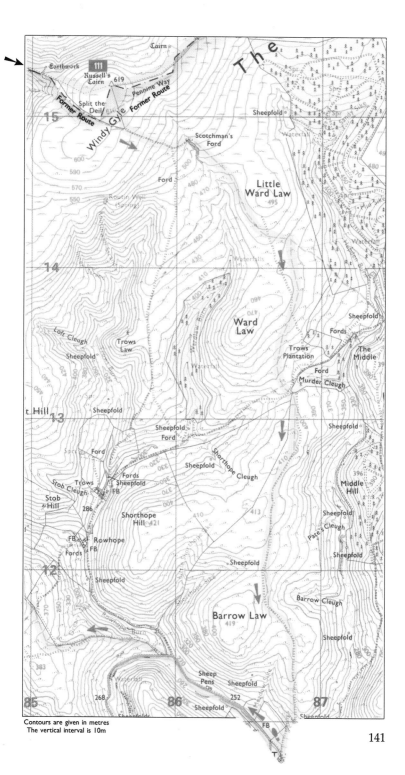

Contours are given in metres
The vertical interval is 10m

141

From the summit, the Way leads north-east on the Scottish side of the fence and descends quite sharply before levelling off at about 1,770 feet (540 metres). After half a mile another old drove road cuts across the ridge at a ladder-stile and gate **M**. This is Clennell Street, which can either be followed north-west to Cocklawfoot or south-east to Uswayford (pronounced Oozyford).

This is the logical halfway point on the Cheviot traverse and you should consider continuing only if you are feeling fit and there are at least six hours' daylight left. Backpackers can overnight here to the lee of the ridge, but for the rest there is an unavoidable detour to find accommodation.

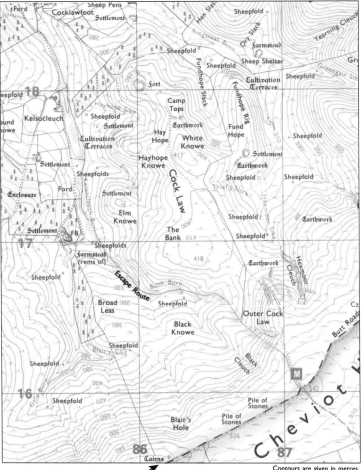

Contours are given in metres
The vertical interval is 10m

Border troubles

The barren state of the Border hills reflects a turbulent episode in Britain's history, beginning with an attack on Scotland by Edward I in 1295 and ending with the Union of the Crowns in 1603. Had this gloriously wild part of Britain never been a frontier, its agriculture would have developed further and faster.

Many armies have fought in the Borders – Romans, Normans, Celts and Anglo-Saxons – but between major conflicts there were long periods of peace during which the rural economy was able to recover. However, the troubles that began in the 14th century rumbled on for too long for anyone to feel secure, and war became a fact of life. Both the land and the people grew impoverished and mean; only the most powerful landowners were able to protect themselves, by building tower houses with massively thick walls. Thirlwall Castle (see page 90) dates from this period.

The most famous Border battle took place in 1388 when Earl Douglas of Scotland gained a victory over the impetuous Harry Hotspur, son of the Earl of Northumberland, in a moonlit encounter on the hill above Otterburn in Redesdale (see page 122). Hotspur gained his revenge in 1402 at the battle of Humbleton Hill in the Cheviots, where he was able to employ Welsh archers to decimate a Scottish army 10,000 strong.

To control the violence in what had become a buffer zone between kingdoms, the Border was split into three zones or marches, each under the wardenship of a lord appointed by the king. There were regular meetings, usually at remote Border crossing points, between the corresponding wardens, but these sometimes degenerated into bloodbaths. The Hanging Stone on the slopes of Cairn Hill (see page 146) marked the boundary of the Middle March and was sometimes used for such meetings, as was Russell's Cairn 111 on Windy Gyle, where Lord Francis Russell was murdered at a wardens' meeting in 1585.

The whole Border area had degenerated by this time into a wasteland. Any remaining vestige of tree cover disappeared, houses were burned to the ground, cattle were stolen and whole families killed by marauding 'reivers' or 'moss-troopers'. The worst areas for this lawlessness were Redesdale and Tynedale on the English side, where the residents were accused of being 'wild and misdemeaned people' who delighted in 'theftes and spoyles'.

Not surprisingly, landowners continued to build their houses with thick walls and call their tenants to the muster roll at the first sign of trouble. 'Pele towers', smaller versions of the tower houses, were widespread by the end of the 15th century – for those who could afford them. One of the best-preserved examples, of a 'vicar's pele', is at Elsdon in Redesdale. In 1555 a defensive zone 20 miles (32 km) wide was established right along the Border, and the inhabitants of the area were obliged to dig ditches to keep out the 'reiving, riding Scots'. Poor farmers built turf cottages which could easily be rebuilt; those with something worth defending built square bastlehouses. These dour grey buildings had walls 3 feet thick and tiny windows. The ground floor was probably used to house cattle and sheep, while the upper floor, accessible only by a heavy trapdoor, provided living quarters for the family.

The worst of the troubles came to an end as a result of the Union of the Crowns in 1603 and the Restoration in 1660. People began to look forward with hope, though new farmhouses were built solid and square, reflecting a lack of trust in human nature and the weather. Old bastles fell derelict, as at Horneystead (see page 106), or were adapted and used as barns or byres, as at Lowstead (see page 106).

It has taken 300 years for the borderlands to recover from the bitter harvest of war. The wide hills and valleys of Northumberland still bear the scars.

The ruins of Thirlwall Castle are probably destined to tumble into the Tipalt Burn one day.

Clennell Street to Kirk Yetholm

11¼ miles (18 km)

CLENNELL STREET   The Schil   Kirk Yetholm

112———114———118———122———123

The Cheviot   Green Humbleton

The course of the Pennine Way embraces some of the best scenery but the worst walking conditions in the Cheviots, and the traverse of the highest ground can be gruelling. This section begins at the Border Gate, a dip in the ridge to the east of Windy Gyle marking the crossing point of the ancient trackway of Clennell Street **112**. It is reached either by walking the Border Ridge, on the Pennine Way, or by climbing from Usway Burn and Coquetdale to the south, or Cocklawfoot to the north-west.

From the Border Gate the Pennine Way keeps to the English side of the Border fence. This is a post and wire affair and seems inappropriate for an international frontier, but there is little or no stone for a wall. The ridge drops away sharply on the greener Scottish side and there are no foreground views; it is the sweep of peatland, of moss and heather, that stays in the memory. England can be a remarkably barren place. A recent plantation of spruce trees has rendered the slopes of the Usway Burn less hostile. Much of this area was once wooded; Scottish raiders in the 14th and 15th centuries were blamed for stealing, bit by bit, this Cheviot forest and by the 18th century nothing was left. The wilderness was a place for outlaws, including the Highlander Black Rory who ran several illicit stills, including one at the foot of Davidson's Burn, to the south-east of King's Seat.

The Way leads north-north-east past the triangulation point at King's Seat **A**, then turns north-east to follow the fence up towards Cairn Hill. The ground is very boggy; hags and sikes can be outmanoeuvred by looking at the lie of the land and detouring to right or left, but progress is slow. Ahead is the great dome of The Cheviot, flanked by lesser hills bearing pimples of rocks or tors, fragments of andesite baked and hardened when the Cheviot granite welled up beneath an extinct volcano nearly 400 million years ago. The ascent towards Cairn Hill is steep and exacting. The little outcrop of rocks on the brow of the hill to the right is the Hanging Stone **113**, which separated the Middle March from the East March in the days when the borderlands were governed by marcher lords. Underfoot the ground is often treacherous and the vegetation is wind-blasted and sheep-cropped. There is bilberry, cowberry and crowberry, none of which manage to produce very much

146

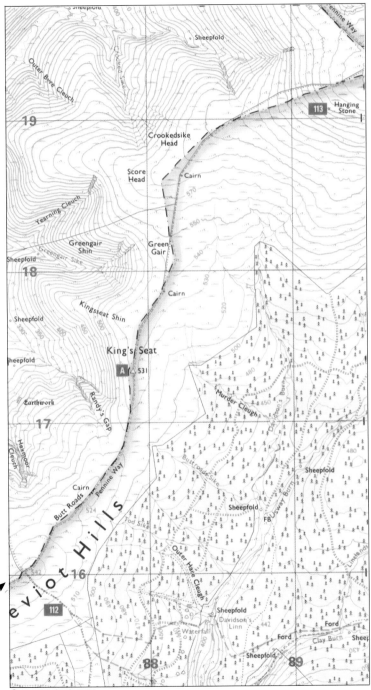

Contours are given in metres
The vertical interval is 10m

147

fruit. There is also a lot of cloudberry, a dwarf relative of the raspberry, which every now and then produces a crop of tasty pink berries.

The top of the hill is an appalling quagmire; picking your way across the morasse it is easy to miss the stile to the left, just after the fences meet at a taller post **B**. Here you must decide whether to include a detour to take in The Cheviot **114**. At 2,674 feet (815 metres) it is a lofty summit but it is topped by an evil blanket of peat and the views are not especially good. The whole whaleback is heavy going and this is only its tail-end. Whatever you decide, the Way continues on its proper course at the stile heading north-west. It then negotiates another quagmire of liquid peat (this is the last bad section on the whole Way; make the most of a scapegoat!). To the right (north-east) is the headwater of the College Burn **115** which scores a course through a cleft in the side of the mountain and disappears from view. A little further on is Auchope Cairn **C**, which must be the most exposed and uncomfortable place on the whole ridge. The only birds likely to be seen here are snow buntings (which are quite regular, at almost any time of the year) and peregrines.

There is a small stone shelter which provides some protection from the wind, but it is a better idea to descend by the north-

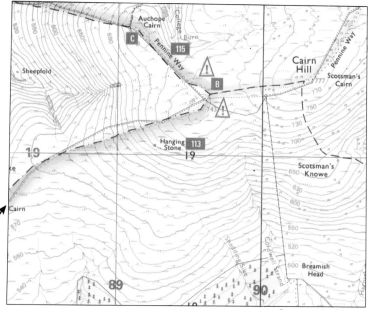

Contours are given in metres
The vertical interval is 10m

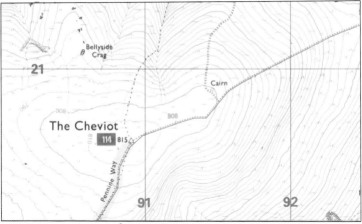

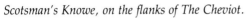

Contours are given in metres
The vertical interval is 10m

Scotsman's Knowe, on the flanks of The Cheviot.

College Valley seen from the Border Ridge at Red Cribs.

west path and make for the more complete shelter **116** provided by a mountain refuge hut – similar to the one at Yearning Saddle on Lamb Hill and a vital sanctuary for anyone caught out by foul weather. From here the Way follows a clear path, still parallel with the Border fence, along a ridge linking 1,640-foot (500-metre) hills. The views are breathtaking, west across green pastures and the Bowmont Water to Windy Gyle, and east to the Hen Hole **117**, a hanging valley formed when the glaciers retreated 10,000 years ago. To the north is the College Valley, reputedly named after a coven of witches, beyond which is the coastal plain and the North Sea. The end of the Pennine Way lies only 7½ miles (12 km) away but this is still a dangerous place, unpredictable to the last. The wreckage of at least two lost aircraft lies on the sides of The Cheviot, and as recently as 1988 two walkers were killed in a snow avalanche on the Bizzle Crag beyond West Hill.

The Schil **118** is the last big hill on the route and one of the finest of all the Cheviot summits. The climb up to it is short and sharp, and the rocky crags on the top provide an exhilarating panoramic view. On the descent on the north side there are several tors (two in particular **119** frame the College Valley and help to make a good photograph). These tors are remnants of a metamorphic aureole, a circlet of hardened rocks, standing sentinel around The Cheviot.

The sweep downhill still follows the Border and leads to a ladder-stile **D** in the wall in a saddle or col between The Schil

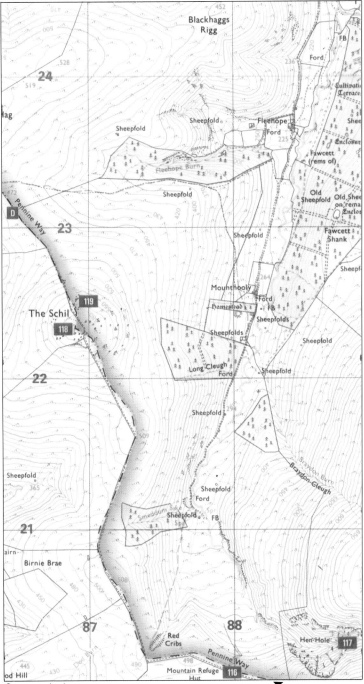

Contours are given in metres
The vertical interval is 10m

151

and Black Hag. After this there is a ladder-stile **E** over the wall to the left; the path to the right leads down to Fleehope and Mounthooly, above the College Burn. It is possible to arrange to be picked up by car from either of these remote farms, for although the 5 mile (8 km) road from Westnewton is private, the College Valley Estate allows a quota of permits for private vehicles. On the full Pennine walk such a deviation would be unthinkable, but pre-planned, an exploration of the valley would make an excellent weekend.

The Way crosses the stile into Scotland; for several miles it will stay a stone's throw from the Border but you will not set foot in England again so this is an important departure. A path leads north-west, below Corbie Craig and above the head of the Rowhope Burn, but after only a few hundred yards the Way forks **F**, either heading back up to the ridge at Steerrig Knowe or over the col between Black Hag and The Curr to the west. This route, which soon resolves itself into a track, then follows a path north along the Halter Burn. It provides an easy descent into Kirk Yetholm, but it is considered passé and is recommended only as a foul-weather alternative. The route favoured by most walkers keeps with the Border Ridge to the very end, to wring the last drop of excitement and endurance from the great walk. Certainly it follows a much more dramatic line, if you are still capable of it. From Steerrig Knowe **G** the Way heads north-north-east, keeping to the grassy ridge of Steer Rig, and losing height all the time. Ahead is the twin-cairned summit of Coldsmouth Hill. To the west are Cheviot foothills and the green fields of the Bowmont. To the east is the bleached, treeless valley of the Trowup Burn **120**; sheep tracks contouring around Saughieside Hill emphasise the wide open spaces and the crazy way nature has of fitting tiny streams into great, ice-worn bowls. The stream itself resembles a pulled thread of wool, braiding or meandering sharply within the confines of its channel.

The terrain is grassy and firm. The last testing climb now lies ahead as the Way turns north-west to White Law **121**. Although of modest height, the slopes are steep, but the summit has a fine outlook, north-west over the Tweed Valley to the Lammermuir Hills and north-east to the Bowmont and the Till. Between these rivers lies Branxton where the Battle of Flodden, the conclusive defeat of the Scots, was fought in 1513. In the far distance is Berwick and the North Sea. To the east are the outer bastions of the Cheviots, above the mouth of the College near Hethpool.

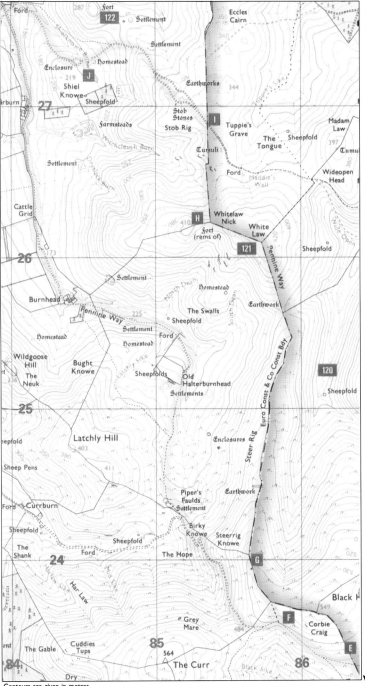

These are Hare Law, Wester Tor, Easter Tor and Yeavering Bell. Yeavering, the most noteworthy of the group, is one of the most important archaeological sites in the Borders. Below it lies the site of the Anglo-Saxon palace of Ad Gefrin where the kings of Northumbria, Aethelfrith and Edwin, held court. The twin-peaked summit of the Bell itself, seen here in profile, is encircled by a stone rampart within which are the traces of 130 circular houses dating back to the Iron Age. (The Eildons, now to the west-north-west, have a similar large hill fort of the Votadini Tribe. These must have been important sites in pre-Roman times.)

Between White Law and Yeavering Bell lies Great Hetha, another Iron Age hill fort. Looking at a map suggests that most suitable hills had settlements of some kind; the population of these uplands was considerably greater 2,000 years ago than it is now. Wild goats, which still roam the slopes between Easter Tor and Yeavering, have seen civilisations wax and wane without making very much of an impression on the land.

The Way has nowhere left to go now and begins its final descent to the Bowmont Valley. Those who are walking just this section may feel a sense of satisfaction; those who have come

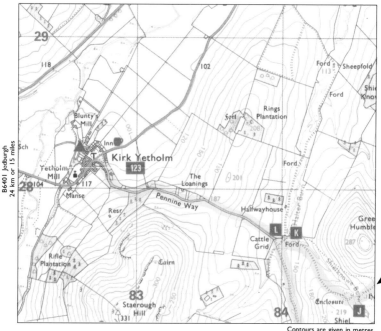

Contours are given in metres
The vertical interval is 10m

from Edale are likely to be beyond sensing anything at all. There is such a little way to go to add to the harvest of memories.

Cross a ladder-stile **H** and head downhill, northwards, alongside a wall until a track goes obliquely left **I**, signed at the wall. From here the Way leaves the Border and drops down along a green track. Ahead to the north-west is Green Humbleton **122**, a grassy hill with another Iron Age hill fort at its crown, but the Way angles south-west around its lower slopes along ancient sheep tracks, then follows the Shielknowe Burn **J** down to meet the Halter Burn **K**.

The whole valley seems very bright and colourful after the hills, and the little Halter Burn, which draws most of its water from the western slopes of Steer Rig, is shallow and easily forded unless there has been very heavy rain on the ridge.

The Way meets a tarmac road at a cattle grid **L** and bears right to follow this west-north-west for the last mile of the journey. In the summer the lane is lined by green hawthorns and by walls dabbed white by lichen. There are banks of red campion and yellow broom and in the evening sunlight the ribbon of road shines gold against indigo shadows. At the end of this rainbow lies the little Border village of Kirk Yetholm **123**, famous now as the terminus of the Pennine Way. The 'finishing line' is generally held to be the sign at the bus stop or the bar of the Border Hotel. Your thoughts about the 250-mile (402-km) trail will depend on how you fared. Whatever the weather was like, no matter how treacherous the route and how tired you are, you will look back with a sense of achievement; you found time for something worth while and were up to the challenge. Someone at Edale may even now be looking to the north, wondering what lies ahead . . .

The Cheviot Hills

When Pennine Way veterans gather together, their most daunting stories tend to centre around the Cheviot bogs. This is not necessarily fair, but there is no doubt that the Cheviot traverse is a challenge, a high-level walk across the least populated hills in the country, often in poor weather and at the end of an exhausting two- or three-week trek. The best way to appreciate the finer points of the Cheviots is by spending a weekend in the area and approaching the Border Ridge from one of the radiating valleys (one of the routes out of Coquetdale is illustrated on page 141).

College Valley from the north slopes of The Schil.

Glimpsed from afar the Cheviot Hills look like a jumble of frosted green domes. In fact they are grouped into a nebula of broad ridges with The Cheviot – a 2,676-foot (815-metre) whaleback of granite – at the heart of the constellation. The history of the Cheviots is quite different from that of the Pennines. They were created by the outpourings of a gigantic system of volcanoes 380 million years ago. The lava cooled to form andesite; at that time the spectacular range of mountains may well have resembled the modern Andes, from which the type of rock has earned its name. When the volcanoes fell silent an upwelling of magma beneath the hills left the Cheviots with a core of granite. Erosion gradually rounded the contours and stripped the covering of andesite from the top of the intrusion so that the highest ground now has several exposures of this harder rock at the surface. Because it cooled slowly deep underground, granite is composed of large crystals (unlike extrusive volcanic rocks like the dolerite of the Whin Sill) which are made up of quartz, feldspar and mica. Where the hot granite touched the andesite it cooked or hardened it. Today, tors of this 'baked' andesite occur as an aureole around the high summits of The Cheviot and Hedgehope, visible on several of the hill crests and slopes to the east of the Pennine Way.

At one time the Cheviots were an island surrounded by a shallow sea, at another they were a headland looking out over an immense river depositing 1,000 feet (300 metres) of sand into a delta to the south and east.

Eventually, rivers worked their way into faults in the massif, and valleys and hills were rounded by glaciers into the present rolling landscape. The andesite covers an area of 350 square miles (900 square km). Although rich in silica it is not so acidic as the granite or the Fell Sandstone to the south, so most of the foothills are covered in grass rather than heather and are called the White Land.

The route of the Pennine Way from Coquethead to Cairn Hill on the shoulder of The Cheviot lies along a broad watershed of peat, but north of the treacherous Auchope mire the ground improves and the stretch from The Schil to White Law is usually perfect. These two conical summits are as attractive and impressive as anything on the whole route, but of course most Pennine Way grafters will by this time have their minds fixed on home and their fund of stories.

PART THREE

USEFUL
INFORMATION

Many of the characteristics that make the Pennine Way such an exciting prospect – the remote terrain, lack of roads and absence of towns – make it extremely difficult to plan a walk, because public transport and accommodation are limited. The following notes are intended as a précis of planning information, referring to more comprehensive services where these are available. Details of transport and accommodation, which will be necessary for planning, are included for the whole of the Pennine Way, north and south. These are followed by details of useful regional addresses and a bibliography of titles of use on the northern half of the Way.

All Pennine Way walkers should be aware of the Pennine Way Council, which exists to protect the Way and to provide information and a forum in which organisations and individuals can get together to discuss matters relating to the Way. Details about associate membership can be obtained from the Secretary, Chris Sainty, 29 Springfield Park Avenue, Chelmsford, Essex, CM2 6EL.

Transport

Finding public transport to or from the towns and villages close to the Way can be a headache. A recent and very welcome innovation is Trans-Pennine Transport. Between 10th June and 10th September it runs a daily Sherpa service: a shuttle of rucksacks (and passengers) from point to point along the Way, so that walkers can collect their gear at their pre-arranged evening stop. A Pennine Way Express (minibus) runs from Kirk Yetholm to Edale and Manchester, calling at Newcastle, Leeds and Sheffield. The rucksack service costs £3 per day (1989 price), while the express from Kirk Yetholm to Sheffield, Edale or Manchester costs £21.50–£24.50. Full details are obtainable from TPT at 3/25 Cathcart Hill, London, N19 5QN. Tel. Skipton (0756) 753146 or London (01) 263 5435 (evenings).

The principal public transport points along the Way are as follows (adapted from the Pennine Way Council booklet):

Edale: trains to and from Manchester and Sheffield. Tel. Manchester (061) 832 8353, the main enquiry office in Manchester.

Crowden: a bus service between Manchester and Sheffield passes Crowden Youth Hostel. Tel. Manchester (061) 236 2120.

Marsden: a train service from Manchester to Huddersfield and Leeds stops at Marsden several times a day.

Standedge: bus services between Huddersfield and Oldham extend to Manchester on Saturday, passing the door of Globe Farm.

Hebden Bridge: the Liverpool–Manchester–Leeds line passes through Hebden Bridge frequently during the week and also has a Sunday service.

Haworth: the private Worth Valley line stops at Haworth. This will take you to the main station at Keighley, to connect with British Rail.

Cowling: Pinnacle Coaches (tel. Cross Hills (0535) 33823) runs a service from Cowling.

Thornton-in-Craven: a Pennine Motors coach (tel. Gargrave (075678) 215) runs between Colne, Earby and Skipton, calling at Thornton-in-Craven. Trains from Colne and Skipton run to Leeds and Manchester.

Gargrave: Pennine Motors runs a service to Gargrave; from here there are buses to Skipton, Settle and Malham.

Malham: tel. Gargrave (075678) 215 for buses to Skipton via Gargrave.

Horton-in-Ribblesdale: a coach runs to Settle via Horton. Tel. Settle (07292) 3235.

Hawes: a bus goes from here to Richmond. You can get a further bus to connect with British Rail at Darlington.

Thwaite and Keld: an infrequent bus service runs to Richmond daily. Tel. Darlington (0325) 468771 to check the times.

Bowes has a once-a-day midweek bus service to Barnard Castle, from where there is an hourly service to Darlington.

Middleton-in-Teesdale has an infrequent bus service to Darlington. Tel. the United Bus Company, Darlington (0325) 468771 for the times.

Dufton: the nearest public transport is at Appleby where there is a station on the Leeds–Settle–Carlisle line.

Alston: Wright Brothers runs coaches from Alston to Haltwhistle via Slaggyford, and from Alston to Penrith. Tel. Alston (0498) 81200.

Greenhead and Twice Brewed: the Carlisle–Newcastle bus runs
hourly through both these places. Tel. Carlisle (0228) 38484
for details.

Bellingham: Tyne Valley Coaches runs a service to Hexham
where you can connect with British Rail to Newcastle.

Byrness: a school bus runs to Bellingham and a City Link runs
daily from Newcastle to Edinburgh. Tel. 031 556 8464.

Kirk Yetholm: Lowland Scottish runs a daily service to Kelso.
Tel. Kelso (0573) 24141. A service runs from Kelso to
Jedburgh, where connections can be made with Newcastle
and Edinburgh.

Accommodation

The Pennine Way Council produces an invaluable *Accommodation and Camping Guide* with up-to-date lists of addresses. This
costs 60p (plus an A5 s.a.e.) and is obtainable from John
Needham, 23 Woodland Crescent, Hilton Park, Prestwich,
Manchester, M25 8WQ.

For anyone planning to stay at youth hostels the Pennine Way
Bureau produces a booklet describing the hostels and runs a
comprehensive booking service (i.e. involving one letter rather
than 17). Contact Pennine Way Bureau, YHA (Yorkshire Area
Office), 96 Main Street, Bingley, West Yorkshire, BD16 2JH.

Members of the Ramblers' Association (address below) will
find some accommodation information in their yearbook.
Otherwise, the best way to book overnight bed and breakfast is
through tourist information centres or national park information centres. These will also have up-to-date lists of camp sites.

Tourist information centres (TICs) are also a useful source of
local information. The following are the TICs in the vicinity of
the Pennine Way:

Glossop TIC, Station Forecourt, Norfolk Street, Glossop,
Derbyshire. Tel. Glossop (04574) 5920.

Hebden Bridge TIC, 1 Bridge Gate, Hebden Bridge, West
Yorkshire, HX7 8JP. Tel. Halifax (0422) 843831.

Haworth TIC, 2/4 West Lane, Haworth, West Yorkshire, BD22
8EF. Tel. Haworth (0535) 42329.

Skipton TIC, 8 Victoria Square, Skipton, North Yorkshire. Tel.
Skipton (0756) 2809.

Settle TIC, Town Hall, Cheapside, Settle, North Yorkshire. Tel.
Settle (07292) 3617.

Horton-in-Ribblesdale TIC, Pen-y-Ghent Café, Horton-in-

Ribblesdale, North Yorkshire, BD24 0HE. Tel. Horton-in-Ribblesdale (07296) 333.

National Park Centre, Station Road, Hawes, North Yorkshire, DL8 3NT. Tel. Hawes (09697) 450.

Brough TIC, The 'One Stop' Shop, Main Street, Brough, Cumbria, CA17 4BL. Tel. Brough (09304) 260.

Appleby-in-Westmorland TIC, The Moot Hall, Borough-gate, Appleby-in-Westmorland, Cumbria, CA16 6YB. Tel. Appleby (07683) 51177.

Alston TIC, The Railway Station, Alston, Cumbria, CA9 3JB. Tel. Alston (0498) 81696.

Haltwhistle TIC, Sycamore Street, Haltwhistle, Northumberland, NE49 0AQ. Tel. Haltwhistle (0498) 20351.

Once Brewed Visitor Centre, Military Road, Barden Mill, Hexham, Northumberland, NE47 7AN. Tel. Barden Mill (04984) 396.

Hexham TIC, Manor Office, Hallgate, Hexham, Northumberland, NE46 1XD. Tel. Hexham (0434) 605225.

Kelso TIC, Turret House, Kelso, Borders Region. Tel. Kelso (0573) 23464.

The principal overnight stopping places on the Way are:

Edale (YH; b & b; camping)
Crowden (YH; camping)
Globe Farm, Standedge (b & b; camping)
Mankinholes (YH)
Lothersdale (b & b; camping)
Malham (YH; b & b; camping; bunkhouse barn)
Horton-in-Ribblesdale (b & b; camping; bunkhouse barn)
Hawes (YH; b & b; camping)
Keld (YH; b & b)
Bowes (b & b; camping)
Baldersdale (YH; limited b & b; camping)
Langdon Beck (YH; b & b)
Dufton (YH; b & b; camping)
Garrigill (b & b; camping; bunkhouse barn)
Alston (YH; b & b; camping)
Greenhead (YH; b & b; camping)
Once Brewed (YH; b & b; camping)
Bellingham (YH; b & b; camping)
Byrness (YH; b & b)
Coquetdale and Uswayford (limited b & b)
Kirk Yetholm (YH; b & b; camping)

Teesdale from above Cronkley.

Useful addresses

Countryside Commission (Headquarters): John Dower House, Crescent Place, Cheltenham, Gloucestershire, GL50 3RA. Tel. Cheltenham (0242) 521381.

Countryside Commission (Northern Region): Warwick House, Grantham Road, Newcastle upon Tyne, Tyne and Wear, NE2 1QF. Tel. Tyneside (091) 2328252.

Durham County Conservation Trust, 52 Old Elvet, Durham, DH1 3HN.

English Heritage (Northern Region): Arnhem Block, The Castle, Carlisle, Cumbria, CA3 8UR. Tel. Carlisle (0228) 31777.

Forestry Commission: Kielder Forest District, Eals Burn, Bellingham, Hexham, Northumberland, NE48 2AJ. Tel. Bellingham (0660) 20242.

National Trust (Northumbria Regional Office): Scot's Gap, Morpeth, Northumberland, NE61 4EG. Tel. Scot's Gap (067074) 691.

Nature Conservancy Council (North Eastern Region): Archbold House, Archbold Terrace, Newcastle upon Tyne, Tyne and Wear, NE1 1EG. Tel. Tyneside (091) 2816316/7.

Nature Conservancy Council (North Western Region): Blackwell, Bowness on Windermere, Cumbria, LA23 3JR. Tel. Windermere (09662) 5286.

Northumberland National Park and Countryside Department: Eastburn, South Park, Hexham, Northumberland, NE46 1BS. Tel. Hexham (0434) 605555.

Northumberland Wildlife Trust: Hancock Museum, Barras Bridge, Newcastle upon Tyne, NE2 2AA. Tel. Tyneside (091) 2320038.

Northumbria Tourist Board: Aykley Heads, Durham, DH1 5UX. Tel. Tyneside (091) 3846905.

Ordnance Survey, Romsey Road, Maybush, Southampton, SO9 4DH. Tel. Southampton (0703) 792763.

Ramblers' Association: 1/5 Wandsworth Road, London, SW8 2XX. Tel. London (01) 582 6878.

Royal Society for the Protection of Birds (Northern Regional Office): 'E' Floor, Milburn House, Dean Street, Newcastle upon Tyne, NE1 1LE. Tel. Tyneside (091) 2324148.

Bibliography

Charlton, B., *The Story of Redesdale* (Northumberland National Park, 1986).

——, *Upper North Tynedale* (Northumbria Water Authority, 1987).

Dobson, R. A. (ed.), *The Geology of North East England* (Natural History Society of Northumberland, 1980).

Hadrian's Wall (Souvenir Guide) (English Heritage, 1987).

Hardy, G., *North to South along the Pennine Way* (Frederick Warne, 1983).

Hopkins, Tony, *Northumberland National Park* (Webb & Bower/ Michael Joseph, 1987).

Newton, R., *The Northumberland Landscape* (Hodder & Stoughton, 1972).

Ordnance Survey Leisure Guides, *Northumbria* (OS and AA, 1987).

Peel, J. H. B., *Along the Pennine Way* (David & Charles, 1972).

Pilton, B., *One Man and his Bog* (Corgi, 1986).

Wainwright, A., *Pennine Way Companion* (Westmorland Gazette, 1968).

——, *Wainwright on the Pennine Way* (Michael Joseph, 1985).

Wright, C. J., *A Guide to the Pennine Way* (Constable, 1987, 4th edition).

Northumberland National Park also produces a series of walks books covering circular routes in the Hadrian's Wall area, Coquetdale and the Cheviot Hills. For further details write to the address on page 166.

Borders Regional Council, Dept of Planning and Development, Melrose, TD6 0SA, has countryside walk cards on the Cheviot Hills section of the Pennine Way.

Ordnance Survey Maps covering the Pennine Way (North)
Landranger Maps: 74, 75, 80, 86, 87, 91, 92.

Pathfinder Maps: 475(NT82/92), 486(NT61/71), 487(NT81/91) 498(NT60/70), 509(NY69/79), 510(NY89/99) 522(NY88/99), 533(NY67/77), 534(NY87/97) 546(NY66/76), 559(NY65/75), 569(NY64/74) 578(NY62/63).

Outdoor Leisure Maps: Map 31, Teesdale.

Motoring Maps: Reach the Pennines using Routemaster Maps 4, 'Central Scotland and Northumberland' and 5, 'Northern England'.

Distance checklist

To help you plan your accommodation along the northern part of the Pennine Way, and to check your progress, the following distances may be helpful.

location	approx. distance from previous location	
	miles	km
Pasture End	0	0
Baldersdale (Blackton)	3.8	6.1
[Bowes/Baldersdale] Bowes Loop	5.8	9.3
Middleton	6.0	9.7
Saur Hill/Langdon Beck	7.7	12.4
Dufton	12.6	20.3
Garrigill	15.5	24.9
Alston	3.9	6.3
Slaggyford	5.6	9.0
Greenhead	10.9	17.5
Steel Rigg/Once Brewed	6.6	10.6
Bellingham	14.8	23.8
Byrness	14.7	23.6
Chew Green	4.9	7.9
Clennell Street	8.8	14.2
Kirk Yetholm (high level)	11.0	17.7
(low level)	11.3	18.2
(detour to The Cheviot)	+ 2.3	3.7